Ancestry of
Alma Marie Swanson née Weidemann (1904-2004)
of Vassar, Michigan

Compiled by Michael Conrad Swanson
2016

Alma Marie Swanson née Weidemann (1904-2004) of Vassar, Michigan

Copyright © 2016 Michael Conrad Swanson

ISBN-13: 978-1535466806
ISBN-10: 1535466804

Printed by CreateSpace, Charleston, South Carolina.

For my daughter, Steph Maj Swanson

Acknowledgments

I would like to acknowledge the many people who contributed their research and time.

There were five professional genealogists. Wiebke Dannenberg of Hamburg, affiliated with the American/Schleswig-Holstein Heritage Society, sent me a report on her Weidemann research in Germany. Martin Sohn of Burow, Germany, researched and compiled the Wolf ancestry in Prussia and Mecklenburg. Two genealogists in Ireland -- Barbara Bingham of Croom and Catriona Crowe at the National Archives of Ireland -- researched Limerick records and produced reports on the Minahan-O'Brien family. Geneva M. Shafer, an archivist at the Williamson County Public Library in Franklin, Tennessee, helped me piece together the Minahan family in America.

Several near and distant relations of Alma Marie Weidemann contributed to this book. Alma worked on her genealogy in the 1970s. Margery Haite, Alma daughter, shared her own extensive research and sent me photos and documents from her personal collection. Mark Swanson, my brother, compiled a Weidemann family history database. He also preserved photographs, documents, and family artifacts. Janine Leifels, a distant cousin living in Demmin, Germany, shared her Wolf family research. Another cousin, Paul-Otto Irmert of Neustadt in Holstein, found where the Weidemanns lived in Neustadt. My late father, Richard Swanson, preserved many old documents, photos, and old family trees.

Lastly, I want to thank Rebecca Swanson and Mark Swanson for reading some sections and making helpful comments.

Michael Conrad Swanson
Franklin, Tennessee
July 2016

Organization of Book

This book is divided into several chapters, including an introduction, three descendant reports, an ancestor chart, an ancestor report, four picture scrapbooks, and an index.

The introduction outlines Alma Marie Weidemann's ancestry in Germany, Ireland, and America.

There are several reports for those who want to delve into the details. Included in the reports are dozens of newspaper articles, biographies, and obituaries. The reports can be hard to navigate for non-genealogists because they use special numbering systems, so I briefly explain the systems before each section.

There are three descendant reports. These reports trace the descendants of Alma's immigrant grandparents in America. Her cousins spread out across the country and lived in such states as Michigan, Pennsylvania, Indiana, New York, Montana, Ohio, South Dakota, North Dakota, and California.

The next chapters contain an ancestor chart and report about Alma's ancestors in Ireland and Germany. The research into Alma's Old Country ancestors occupied many people for many years, and there is still much to discover.

Lastly, there are four picture scrapbooks followed by a location and name index.

Table of Contents

Table of Contents

Introduction

Alma Marie Swanson née Weidemann's long life was punctuated by early tragedy, but she overcame the loss of her parents to earn a degree, teach, and raise a family. She was a second-generation American: all four of her grandparents were immigrants. Two came from Germany and two from Ireland, immigrating around the time of the American Civil War. Her paternal grandmother, Maria Wolf, came with her family from Germany in 1858. Alma's paternal grandfather, artist Christian Weidemann, came with his brother in 1866. Her maternal grandparents, Mary O'Brien and John Minahan, arrived about 1866 from Ireland.

What caused them to emigrate? What did they do when they arrived in America? Where did they live in the Old World? Who were their ancestors? This book tries to answer these questions.

Wolf/Wolff from Pomerania, Prussia

On June 16, 1858, Abraham Lincoln accepted the Republican nomination for the United States Senate and spoke these historic words: "A house divided against itself cannot stand. I believe this government cannot endure, permanently, half slave and half free."

One week earlier -- on June 7, 1858 -- the Wolf family walked off the sailing ship *Donau* docked in New York City. They took their first steps on solid ground since the ship left Hamburg five weeks earlier. One of their children was sixteen-year-old Maria Wolf, Alma Weidemann's future paternal grandmother.

Lincoln's words had meaning for the Wolfs. Their ancestors in Pomerania and Mecklenburg were enslaved on feudal estates and sold like property to other noblemen. When the serfs were freed in the early 1800s, the laws in the region prohibited peasants from having permanent residences. So they traveled from town to town and estate to estate trying to earn enough to eat, homeless between jobs.

In 1858, the year the Wolfs emigrated, the poet Fritz Reuter penned these lines about the worsening plight of Mecklenburg peasants, who felt betrayed by their country and former lords:

> And none will give us housing (rights)
> Here under our own (safe) 'heaven'
> No place for us, for me and you?
> No place in our native land
> We are shown such disgraceful faithlessness

On May 1, 1858, the Wolf family boarded the *Donau*, a three-masted sailing ship, in Hamburg. Carl Wolf and Elizabeth Hillmann brought their eight children. The youngest child on board was two-year-old Wilhelm Wolf. The eldest child was Elizabeth's biological son and Carl's stepson, twenty-four-year-old Johann Conrad.

Maria Wolf was born in Wolkow, Pomerania in 1841. Wolkow is a tiny village in northeast Germany about sixty miles west of Poland at what was then the border of Mecklenburg and Pomerania. The German Empire at the time was comprised of many nation-states of various foreign affiliations. Germany would not be a u nified nation until 1871.

Their surname was spelled several ways in Germany, usually Wolf and Wulf, but they consistently spelled it Wolff in America. The Wolfs spoke Low German, the main dialect in northern Germany during the nineteenth century. The dialect is closer to Dutch than standard German.

Maria's ancestors lived in the villages of Wolkow (Pomerania), Kastorf (Mecklenburg), Fouquettin (Pomerania), Wolde (Mecklenburg), Galenbeck (Mecklenburg), Zwiedorf (Pomerania), and Wildberg (Pomerania), among others. These villages surround a lake called Kastorfer See and today are known for their old churches, expansive feudal mansions, and the ruins of castles and forts. The ruins of three seventh-century Slavic settlements, perhaps the oldest in the area, are on the north shore of Kastorfer See.

The earliest ancestors found for Maria Wolf were her second great-grandparents, Catherina Ebert

Introduction

and Thomas Brüggert who were married in 1755 in Kastorf. They were serfs on the estate of the family von Kalden.

Their child, Maria Brüggert, married Johann Teage in 1782 in Kastorf.

Their child, Christina Teage, married Carl Wolf in 1810 in Zwiedorf.

Their child, the younger Carl Wolf, was born in 1814 in Zwiedorf. He married Elisabeth Hillman, who was born in Galenbeck and baptized in Kastorf in 1811. Before emigrating, Carl Wolf moved his family from Wolkow to Fouquettin and finally to Wildberg.

Several generations suffered through invasions of their homeland. In 1805, Russian troops passed though Mecklenburg, leaving destruction in their wake. One year later, Napoleon Bonaparte conquered and plundered Prussia and Mecklenburg. The French were defeated in the Wars of Liberation in 1813.

In 1820, serfdom was abolished in the area, but a post-war economic depression forced some feudal lords to release serfs earlier. After the serfs were emancipated, the manor lords destroyed the peasants' homes to increase their cropland. This period was known as "the peasant seizure" when thousands of peasants in the area lost their holdings. The peasants were free, but suddenly homeless.

Maria's father, the younger Carl Wolf, was a weaver following the occupation of his father. Carl Wolf's search for steady work forced him to move from village to village. By the mid-1800s, linen weavers like Carl were being put out of business by foreign competition and mechanical looms. There was little choice but to emigrate.

On June 7, 1858, Carl and his family arrived in America. "Landing at New York they pushed on westward to Wayne County, Michigan, buying a tract of land fourteen miles west of Detroit. A log cabin and a small cleared space constituted the improvements. The log cabin was the first home of the Wolff family in America. Carl Wolff gave his time to clearing the land and tilling the soil. There was but little demand for either wood or lumber, and great maple logs were rolled together and burned. Some years later the Wolff family moved to the southwestern corner of Michigan in Berrien County, where Carl Wolff bought an eighty acre farm in Buffalo Township." (*Indiana and Indianans,* 1918)

Carl and Elisabeth Wolff, with their son John Conrad, secured a mortgage for a farm in Nankin near Detroit. When they moved west to New Buffalo, Berrien County, Michigan, their three daughters -- Augusta, Maria, and Carolina -- remained in the Detroit area. Augusta married a butcher, Peter Eberle; Maria married an artist, Christian Weidemann; Carolina, and her husband, Carl Bewernitz, took over the Wolff farm in Nankin.

The farm in New Buffalo, about two blocks from Lake Michigan, grew to 160 acres. John Conrad took over the farm from his step-father, Carl, when Carl retired to nearby Michigan City, Indiana.

Three of the Wolffs' sons -- Charles, Edmund, and William -- left the family farm in New Buffalo and headed for the "wild frontier." The first to leave was eighteen-year-old Charles, who traveled by wagon train to California about 1866. He returned to Michigan in 1868, but headed west again to work for the Northern Pacific Railroad. In 1870 he owned a cattle ranch near Bismarck, Dakota Territory. From 1873 through 1876 he drove a supply wagon for General Custer, and was driving one of his supply wagons on the day of his Last Stand. "Mr. Wolff was also with General Custer's freight train in 1876 when Custer was on his last expedition. The general and his troops left the train at midnight, and the following day were beset by the Indians and massacred practically to a man. The freight train had a guard of forty soldiers and started at daylight, but after going about a mile was surrounded by Indians, and a halt was called and the soldiers and drivers dug themselves in and stood a siege for two weeks before being relieved by General Crook and taken to the Black Hills." (*Indiana and Indianans,* 1918)

Charles's brother, Edmund, moved to Lawrence County, Dakota Territory in 1876 or 1877 where he bought ranches just east of Crook City and later in nearby Spearfish. A few miles from Crook City was the lawless mining town of Deadwood, where Wild Bill Hickok was shot and killed in 1876 while playing poker. Edmund retired to Detroit in 1924. Two years later he returned to Deadwood as a

Introduction

tourist to visit the spot where "Preacher Smith" was murdered on his Sunday walk from Crook City to Deadwood.

William (who took "Wallace" as his middle name), also went west to the Dakotas in 1876. He was a freight wagon driver hauling supplies on a route from Bismarck to Crook City and Deadwood. He was a rancher with his brother, Charles, on Charles's Bismarck ranch, and with his brother, Edmund, on Edmund's Crook City ranch. About 1880 he moved to Miles City, Montana by wagon where he became a sheep rancher. By the 1900s he had one of the largest Montana herds on ranges along Beaver Creek and the Tongue River. William also encountered Indians: "[William Wolff] was overseeing a large band of beef steers his brother had near Crook City, and it was his custom to ride out, about eight miles, to the camp of the herders to see how things were progressing, once a week. On one occasion, he was accompanied by two friends and the herders warned them to be careful in their return as Indians were skulking around and were hostile. Accordingly they remained in the camp until sundown when they started on their journey back. Their path led them down the famous Whitewood gulch and as they were progressing along this portion they were suddenly fired upon by the savages. The first volley killed one of their number, all of their horses, wounded our subject in the knee and his surviving companion through the hips. Fortunately they escaped being pinned down by the falling horses and were enabled to crawl to a clump of trees. Although the Indians continued to fire upon them they did not receive another bullet while they were making for cover. Mr. Wolff had a rifle and his companion a six-shooter. The rifle, however, became filled with snow in the fall and could not be used at once. The Indians kept up a bombardment and as often as one showed himself in the least, the six shooter did duty to bring him down. Finally our subject got his rifle into trim and the work began in earnest. Several of the Indians were killed and finally after a couple of hour's continuous firing, they gave up the battle and carried off their dead." (*Illustrated History of Yellowstone Valley*, 1907)

Their sister, Maria Wolff (Alma's grandmother), meanwhile, was living a peaceful life in Detroit, married to Christian Weidemann, where they had nine children. One of Christian and Maria's sons, Oscar Weidemann (Alma's father), would marry Mary Moynahan.

Weidemann from Holstein

On April 9, 1865, General Lee surrendered to the Union and less than a week later Lincoln was assassinated. On June 13, 1866, the United States Congress approved the Fourteenth Amendment granting citizenship and equal rights to freed slaves.

Three weeks later -- on July 6, 1866 -- brothers Christian and Heinrich Weidemann stepped off the sailing ship *Apollo* into New York City, ending a seven-week sea voyage from Hamburg. Twenty-nine-year-old artist Christian Weidemann would be Alma's paternal grandfather.

Christian was born in 1837 in the Baltic coastal town of Neustadt ("new town") in Holstein, in the far north of Germany.

The surname Weidemann (pronounced VIDE-a-man) means "pasture man" in Low German, the predominant dialect in Holstein. This surname fits the area, since Holstein was known for cattle and pasture land. The breed of black-and-white dairy cow known as the American Holstein originated in Holstein and nearby northern Holland.

The earliest ancestors found for Christian Weidemann were his sixth great-grandparents, Margreth Bück and Hans Muuß (b. about 1655). They were married in 1678 at St. Laurentius Church in Süsel, Holstein. St. Laurentius is a twelfth-century church still in use today. They lived in Roge, a village near Neustadt, on the feudal estate called Övelgönne owned by the nobleman Christoph von Rantzau.

In 1686, Rantzau executed eighteen of his serfs for witchcraft. He did so without evidence, in violation of the law. He freed some of his serfs as a bid for clemency, but their freedom was revoked after Rantzau was convicted and forced to sell his three estates. The Dutch nobleman, Johann Georg von Dernath, bought Övelgönne estate in 1695.

Introduction

The Muuß's daughter Engel married Hans Weidemann (b. circa 1680). Hans worked a plot of land in the rural village of Kassau, five miles northwest of Neustadt. His family attended the Basilika Altenkrempe, a thirteenth-century church still in use. Both Kassua and the church were within the expansive feudal estate called Sierhagen, also owned by the family von Dernath. The estate was purchased by the families von Brockdorff in 1730 and von Thienen in 1765. The Sierhagen manor buildings have been restored and are now event venues.

After Hans Weidemann (b. circa 1680), the next four generations of Weidemanns were also born on the Sierhagen estate.

Hans and Engel's son, Hans (b. 1714), had a plot in Stolpe with his wife Maria Schumacher.

Hans and Maria's son, Hans (b. 1748), had a plot in Stolpe with his wife Anna Schumacher. Hans became a landowner about 1793 when serfs were gaining their freedom in the region. His brother, who escaped Sierhagen in 1780, returned home after serfdom was abolished, but remained landless, perhaps sacrificing any claim to land when he escaped.

Hans and Anna's son, Claus (b. 1780), was a farmhand living in Kassau with his wife Anna Haack.

Claus and Anna's son, Claus (b. 1801), was born a free man in Stolpe. He moved five miles south to the town of Neustadt, married Anna Hedewig in 1824, and they had at least eight children there, including Christian and Heinrich Weidemann.

Neustadt, called "Neustadt in Holstein" to distinguish it from the many German towns of the same name, was established in 1244 by Count Adolf IV of Holstein and would soon became a busy port for ships sailing to and from Scandinavia. The town was surrounded by a wall with three gates that corresponded to the town's three quarters. Kemper Tor, the northern gate, stood (and still stands) at the end of Kemper Strasse (Kemper Street) in the second quarter. It was built in 1244 and is the last surviving of the original three town gates. The brick gothic church on Neustadt's central marketplace square is the oldest building in town. An atlas published in 1822 describes Neustadt as "a town in the south of Denmark, in the duchy of Holstein, on the bay of Lubeck. It suffered greatly from the fire in September 1817. Population 1400."

Claus Weidemann and his family lived in the third quarter of Neustadt, probably on a street called Waschgraben. Claus was a laborer, but his sons were apprenticed into trades. His eldest son, Jakob, apprenticed as a cigar maker and opened a shop on Kremper Strasse. Heinrich was apprenticed as a typesetter and Christian was trained as an artist. Their mother, Anna, died when they were not yet teenagers, and their father, Claus, later moved in with a family on Kremper Strasse.

The years from 1848 to 1866 were a period of economic and political turmoil in the northern-most German states, Schleswig and Holstein. The First Schleswig War from 1848-1850 was a fight for Holstein and Lauenburg's independence from Denmark. In the Second Schleswig War in 1864, Prussian and Austrian armies defeated the Danes. The Austro-Prussian War in the summer of 1866 brought Holstein under sole Prussian control. These wars inspired Heinrich Weidemann to write and publish poems and songs about independence.

During this time, Christian and Henrich Weidemann traveled between German states to find stable employment. In 1866, Christian wrote a letter from Hamburg to Heinrich in Lauenburg where he was struggling to start a newspaper. They agreed to leave together for America. On May 15, 1866, Heinrich and Christian boarded the sailing ship *Apollo* in Hamburg. They arrived in New York City seven weeks later and moved in with their sister, Maria Hensler, in Detroit.

Heinrich Weidemann became a printer for a German-language newspaper, *Detroiter Abend*. Christian was a fresco painter, decorator, and project supervisor for the William Wright Company in Detroit. He married Maria Wolff in Detroit in 1868.

Here is the immediate family of Christian Weidemann and Maria Wolff, reconstructed from the research:

Introduction

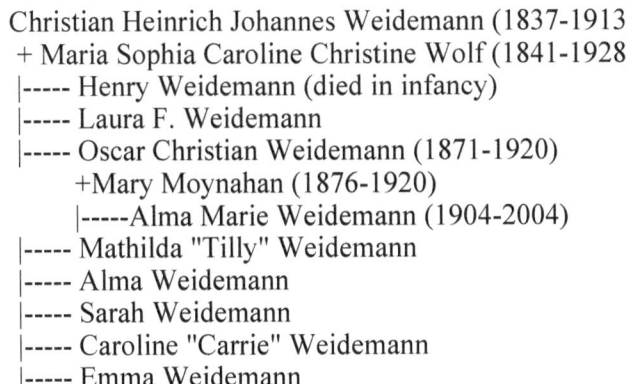

Christian Heinrich Johannes Weidemann (1837-1913)
+ Maria Sophia Caroline Christine Wolf (1841-1928)
|----- Henry Weidemann (died in infancy)
|----- Laura F. Weidemann
|----- Oscar Christian Weidemann (1871-1920)
    +Mary Moynahan (1876-1920)
    |-----Alma Marie Weidemann (1904-2004)
|----- Mathilda "Tilly" Weidemann
|----- Alma Weidemann
|----- Sarah Weidemann
|----- Caroline "Carrie" Weidemann
|----- Emma Weidemann
|----- Walter Weidemann

Of Maria Wolff and Christian Weidemann's nine children, seven survived to adulthood. They worked in a variety of careers: there were two milliners, a decorator, two teachers, a stenographer, and an auto factory engineer.

Laura was a milliner. She married an accountant, Edmund von der Heide, and they had three children.

Oscar followed in his father's footsteps and became a decorator and painter.

Oscar's sister, Alma, was a milliner and a department store salesperson in Detroit. She became guardian to Oscar's daughter, Alma Weidemann, in 1920.

Mathilda was a teacher trainer at Washington Normal School, a teachers' college in Detroit. She was later principal of several schools in the Detroit public school system. Mathilda preserved her father's library of German classics and donated them to the Detroit Public Library.

Caroline was a stenographer in Detroit. She married George Dingledey.

Emma was a teacher in Detroit.

Walter was an automobile factory tool maker and engineer. He married twice, to Laura Lichtenberg and Clara Diem. In 1936, Walter was locked in his car trunk by two carjackers who used his car to commit at least one robbery. Walter escaped six hours later.

Minahan/Moynahan from Limerick, Ireland

In 1854, John Minahan and Mary O'Brien were married at Saint Mary's Immaculate Conception Church in Croom, County Limerick. The church was built in the 1820s and is adjacent to Croom Castle.

Their first four children -- Michael, Patrick, Joseph (who died in infancy), and a second Joseph -- were baptized at St. Mary's.

Croom is a small village fifteen miles south of Limerick City in southwest Ireland. Nearby villages include Adare (known for thatched cottages), Grange (known for the largest stone circle in Ireland), and Partickswell (known for the well that was blessed by St. Patrick).

The River Maigue runs through Croom. In the ninth and tenth centuries Vikings sailed inland to Croom to create alliances with the local Norman rulers, the O'Donovans. The O'Donovan family built Croom Castle in the thirteenth century. The original castle is in ruins, but a rebuilt section is now a private residence

Croom is best known as the birth-place of the "Limerick Poem." In the eighteenth century, dozens of part-time, Gaelic-language wordsmiths called the Maigue Poets regularly converged on Croom to read their work. It is said that the first Limerick was performed at a poetry "court" in a tavern on the fair-green, a field near the castle. The tavern owner, Sean O'Tuama, began with this verse:

Introduction

I sell the best Brandy and Sherry
To make all my customers merry,
But at times their finances
Run short as it chances,
And then I feel very sad, very.

Poet Andrias MacCraith replied:

O'Tuama! You boast yourself handy,
At selling good ale and bright Brandy
But the fact is your liquor
Makes everyone sicker,
I tell you this I your good friend, Andy.

Research has not yet uncovered the identity of John's and Mary's parents, despite the efforts of two professional genealogists. The researchers encountered several problems including the local popularity of their names, the destruction of local census records in a 1922 Dublin bomb blast, and the omission of parents' names on marriage records. One genealogist found a Michael Moynihan, possibly John's father, living at Croom Castle and employed as its gardener; however, more evidence is needed to make a solid connection. On an optimistic note, if John's and Mary's exact birthdates are ever discovered, their Irish baptism records will list their parents.

The surnames Minahan and O'Brien are quite common in County Limerick. Minahan (pronounced MINE-a-han) is an anglicized version of the Gaelic name *Ua Muimhneachain* (pronounced uh-MUV-na-han), which means "male descendant of the Munsterman." County Limerick is in the province of Munster. Other forms of the surname, often used interchangeably, include Moynahan, Moynihan, Minihan, and Monahan. They favored Moynahan in America.

The surname O'Brien comes from the Gaelic name *Ua Briain* (pronounced uh-BREE-an), which means "male descendant of Brian." The name suggests a possible connection to Brian Boru (b. 941), King of Munster and High King of Ireland. Part of Croom is in the barony of Pubblebrien, established by Brian Boru's tenth great-grandson, Brian Dubh Ua Briain. So it is possible, but not at all established, that Mary O'Brien has a drop of royal blood.

In 1845, the Great Famine hit Croom and all of Ireland. A million people starved during the seven-year disaster. Hundreds of famine victims in Croom were buried at the Anhid graveyard. A teacher in Croom who witnessed the horror wrote: "The deaths in my native place were many and horrible. The poor famine-stricken people were found by the wayside, emaciated corpses, partly green from eating docks and nettles and partly blue from the cholera and dysentery." (*Famine Echoes - Folk Memories of the Great Irish Famine, 1995*)

John Minahan and Mary O'Brien were teenagers during the Great Famine. After the famine, many people remained unemployed, which may explain why some of John and Mary's friends and relatives were arrested for protests against the government and for drunkenness, and why at least two of them -- one a witness at their wedding and another their child's godparent -- died in the Croom workhouse.

John and Mary survived the Great Famine, but as Catholics their opportunities were severely limited by the British government. They became part of the massive post-famine flight from Ireland caused by religious oppression, rising rents, and poverty.

Train service came to Croom in 1862, making it easier to travel to the sea port in County Cork. John and Mary left Ireland between 1865 and 1867; however, no ship passenger list has been found to document their departure from Ireland or arrival in America. On August 29, 1868, their child, Thomas Francis, was born in Mt. Vernon, Westchester County, New York. He was baptized on September 6, 1868 at the Immaculate Conception Church in Tuckahoe. His baptism was the first recorded by the church.

Introduction

According to ship passenger lists, Mary traveled back to Ireland in 1868 and 1869, returning both times on the *S.S. Virginia* with some of her children. The journey by steam ship between Queenstown (now Cobh), Cork, Ireland and New York took about a week.

In 1870, John was employed as a stonecutter near the Tuckahoe quarry, a major producer of marble. Hundreds of laborers -- Irish, Italian, German, and African-American -- worked at the quarry after the Civil War. Skilled stonecutters like John made three times the wages of unskilled quarrymen. Cut marble was loaded onto ships at a nearby Hudson River wharf.

In the 1870s, the family moved to Hartford to help build the Connecticut capitol building. By 1876 they had moved back to Westchester County where their daughter, Mary (Alma's mother) was born. No birth or baptismal record has been found.

In late 1876 the family moved to Albany where John and his older sons began work on the New York state capitol building, already in the ninth year of construction. John's wife, Mary, died in 1879 in Albany, leaving him to raise several young children. A family in the same house cared for his youngest daughter, Mary. Two of their sons, John and Thomas, were not found in the Albany census and may have been taken in by friends. The other sons became skilled stonecutters, stone carvers, and sculptors who moved from city to city to help construct hotels, schools, churches, government buildings, and monuments. When the men left Albany for new work, Mary stayed behind with the McNamara family.

John's sons Michael and Joseph formed an architectural stone carving business in Boston called "The Moynahan Brothers." In the late 1890s, John and his sons Michael and William lived in Washington, D.C. where they worked on the Library of Congress.

William traveled widely for stone carving work. His obituary states he "was born in New York City, coming from a family that for several generations had been engaged in sculpting and carving and many fine examples of his work are to be seen in and around Cleveland. While still in the east, before locating in Ohio some twenty odd years ago, he did some outstanding work for the Yale and Duke Universities, and for the Library of Congress, at Washington." (*Stone Cutters' Journal*, 1938)

Here is the immediate family of John Minahan/Moynahan and Mary O'Brien, showing Alma's place in the tree:

```
John Minahan (b. abt 1832-?)
+Mary O'Brien (b. abt 1832--1879)
|-----1. Michael E. Minahan
|-----2. Patrick Minahan
|-----3. Joseph Minahan (infant death)
|-----4. Joseph Minahan
|-----5. John Moynahan
|-----6. Thomas Francis Moynahan
|-----7. May Moynahan
|-----8. William S. Moynahan
|-----9. Edward T. Moynahan
|-----10. Mary Moynahan (1876-1920)
        +Oscar Christian Weidemann (1871-1920)
        |-----Alma Marie Weidemann (1904-2004)
```

Michael, Patrick, Joseph, and William became stone carvers and stonecutters.

Michael and his wife, Margaret McIntyre, had three children in Westchester County, New York. Michael is buried in Sleepy Hollow Cemetery.

William adopted his wife's children and they made a home in Ohio.

May, it is thought, was a domestic servant in New York City.

Mary married Oscar Weidemann and they moved to Erie, Pennsylvania and later to Detroit,

Introduction

Michigan.

Alma and Her Parents

Oscar Weidemann was born in 1871 and grew up in Detroit. From 1891 to 1893 he studied art in New York and won a scholarship for a year in Germany at the Royal Academy of Art in Berlin. While in Germany he visited his family's hometown, Neustadt in Holstein. When he returned, he started a decorating business in Erie, Pennsylvania about 1901.

Mary Moynahan was born in in 1876 in New York, probably in Westchester County. Later that year the Moynahan family moved to Albany. Her mother died there in 1879, and Mary was cared for by the Lardner family who were living in the same house as her widowed father John Moynahan and her older siblings. When her father left Albany, she stayed with the McNamara family.

It is not known how Oscar and Mary first met, but they were married in Buffalo, New York in 1901. After their daughter, Alma, was born in Erie in 1904, they moved to Detroit in 1905 where Oscar worked as a painter with his father.

In 1820, Alma's father shot and killed her mother and himself with a revolver. Parentless at fifteen, she was taken in by her father's sister (also named Alma Weidemann).

Alma graduated from Michigan State Normal School, now Eastern Michigan University, in Ypsilanti and worked as a physical education teacher in the Detroit public school system. In 1928 she married Ewald Swanson. They settled in Vassar, Michigan, where they raised three children, Shirley, Richard, and Margery. Alma passed away in 2004 at the age of 100.

Ancestor Picture Tree

Christian Heinrich Johannes
Weidemann
(1837-1913)

Maria Sophia Caroline Christine
Wolf
(1841-1928)

John Minahan

(circa 1834-   )

Mary O'Brien

(circa 1834-1879)

Oscar Christian Weidemann

(1871-1920)

Mary E. Moynahan

(1876-1920)

Alma Marie Weidemann

(1904-2004)

Maps

Last Places of Residence Before Immigration

Ireland

John Minahan and Mary O'Brien emigrated from Croom, County Limerick, Ireland.

Maps

Last Places of Residence Before Immigration

Germany

The Weidemanns emigrated from Neustadt in Holstein and the Wolfs emigrated from Wildberg on the boarder of Mecklenburg amd Prussia.

Descendant Reports Explained

The first set of reports is about Alma Marie Weidemann's immigrant ancestors and three lines of descent converging to Alma. The Weidemann/Wolf report starts with Christian Weidemann who arrived 1866 on the *Apollo* and Maria Wolf who arrived 1858 on the *Donau*. The second report starts with Maria Wolf's father Carl Wolf and Eisabeth Hillmann who arrived together in 1858 on the *Donau*. The third report starts with John Minahan and Mary O'Brien who arrived about 1866 from Ireland. These reports contain numerous extracts from newspapers and history books including biographies and obituaries.

Each generation has its own subsection. Children who appear in subsequent subsections are assigned numbers. Underlined numbers are assigned to Alma Marie Weidemann's direct ancestors.

Weidemann/Wolf in America

First Generation

1. Christian Heinrich Johannes Weidemann,[1] son of **Claus Friederich Weidemann**[1] and **Anna Catherina Hedewig Ahrend**,[1] was born on 26 Feb 1837 in Neustadt, Ostholstein, Holstein,[2] died on 22 Jun 1913 in Detroit, Wayne, Michigan,[3] and was buried on 25 Jun 1913 in Woodlawn Cemetery, Detroit, Wayne, Michigan.[4] The cause of his death was apoplexy.

General Notes: Born in Neustadt in Holstein, he lived in Austria before coming to America in 1866 with his brother. He worked for Wright and Company, a nationally-known design firm, which provided interior design and architecture services for large homes, commercial buildings, and government buildings. He worked as a fresco painter and supervised large projects including the interior decoration of the Michigan capitol building.

Noted events in his life were:
- Resided: on Waschgraben, circa 1846, Neustadt, Ostholstein, Holstein.[5] The family probably resided on Waschgraben, which is east of the church in the 3rd quarter. Oscar Weidemann made a sketch of the house when he visited Neustadt in 1894.

- Resided: about 1860, Vienna, Austria.[6]

- Occupation: painter, before 1866, Hamburg.[7]

- Emigration: 15 May 1866, Hamburg.[8] on the bark *Apollo* with his brother Henry

- Immigration: 6 Jul 1866, New York, New York, New York.[9] on the *Apollo*

- Occupation: fresco painter, 1870, Detroit, Wayne, Michigan.[10]

- Occupation: fresco painter, 1877, Detroit, Wayne, Michigan.[11]

- Occupation: fresco painter residing downtown at 44 Croghan (Monroe) near Cadillac Square, 1880, Detroit, Wayne, Michigan.[12]

- Occupation: decorating supervisor with William Wright Co. at the state capitol building, about 1888-1889, Lansing, Ingham, Michigan.[13]

- Occupation: decorator, 1900, Detroit, Wayne, Michigan.[14]

- Home Built: from The Detroit Free Press, 16 Apr 1905, Detroit, Wayne, Michigan.[15]

    Architects Norval Wardrop and Louis Keil have prepared plans and have let contracts for a residence for Christian Weidemann, on the north side of Erskine street, between John R. and Brush streets. It is to be a solid paving brick house, slate root, galvanized cornice, hardwood finish for the interior and hardwood floors in the principal rooms, hot water for heating, combination lighting, mantels and modern sanitary plumbing. The dimensions are 32x50. The following contracts have been awarded: Mason work, LeMay & Whelun; carpenter, George Watt; plumbing and heating, John F. Jones; plastering, Gustay Jahnke; painting, William Wright Co.

- Occupation: master painter, 1910, Detroit, Wayne, Michigan.[16]

Weidemann/Wolf

- Resided: 93 Erskine, 1913, Detroit, Wayne, Michigan.[17]

- Cause of death: apoplexy, 22 Jun 1913.[4]

- Obituary: from the Detroit Free Press, 23 Jun 1913.[18]

  > Christian Weidemann, Aged Designer, Dies
  > Succumbs to Heart Disease Sunday Monday at his Detroit Home.
  > Christian Weideman, 75 years old, for more than 40 years connected with the firm of William Wright & Co., as a designer, dies suddenly early Sunday morning at his home, 93 Erskine street, of heart disease.
  > Mr. Weideman was in his usual health when he retired Saturday night but complained about 2:30 a. m. of being ill and later died.
  > Mr. Weideman, along with work on other public buildings, superintended the decoration of the state capitol at Lansing about 20 years ago.
  > The funeral will be held Wednesday at 2 p. m. from the house and burial will be private.
  > Mr. Weideman was born in Neustadt, Germany, in 1837, and came to Detroit about 45 years ago. His first employment in Detroit was with William Wright and he continued with him until his death. As the firm went through various changes in ownership, management and name, Mr. Weideman acquired a financial interest.
  > He is survived by a widow and seven children, Oscar, Mathilde, assistant principal of the Detroit Normal School, Alma Caroline, Emma, Walter and Mrs. E. Von der Heide.

Christian married **Maria Sophia Caroline Christine Wolf,** daughter of **Johann Carl Friedrich Theodor "Carl" Wolf** and **Johanna Sophia Elisabeth "Elizabeth" Hillmann,** on 6 Feb 1868 in Detroit, Wayne, Michigan.[19] Maria was born on 3 Aug 1841 in Wolkow, Wildberg, Pommern, Preußen,[20] was christened on 12 Sep 1841 in Wolkow, Wildberg, Pommern, Preußen,[21] and died on 14 Mar 1928 in Detroit, Wayne, Michigan.[22] Another name for Maria was Mary Wolff.

Christening Notes: Sponsors were: 1. girl Christine Wolf, Schossow, 2. girl Sophie Wolf, Schossow, 3. girl Henriette Hillmann, Galenbeck, 4. wife Johanna Feul, Galenbeck, 5. Joachim Ehrenreich, Wolde, 6. Johann Sievert, Wolkow, 7. bricklayer Martin Tessin, Japzow.

Noted events in her life were:
- Emigration: 1 May 1858, Hamburg.[23] on the bark *Donau*.

- Immigration: 7 Jun 1858, New York, New York, New York.[9]

- Resided: at 44 Croghan (Monroe), 1880, Detroit, Wayne, Michigan.[12]

- Resided: 116 Monroe, 1900, Detroit, Wayne, Michigan.[14]

- Resided: 93 Erskine, 1910, Detroit, Wayne, Michigan.[16] 7 of 8 children living.

- Resided: 93 Erskine, 1920, Detroit, Wayne, Michigan.[24]

- Fact: Home renumbered from 93 to 269 Erskine, 1921, Detroit, Wayne, Michigan.[25]

Weidemann/Wolf

Children from this marriage were:

    i. **Henry Weidemann**[26] was born on 9 Nov 1868 in Detroit, Wayne, Michigan,[27] died on 10 Aug 1869 in Detroit, Wayne, Michigan,[27] and was buried in Woodlawn Cemetery, Detroit, Wayne, Michigan.

    Burial Notes: Buried first at Elmwood Cemetery, then moved to Woodlawn.

2   ii. **Laura F. Weidemann**[26] was born on 13 Dec 1869 in Detroit, Wayne, Michigan[28] and died on 21 Dec 1941 in Detroit, Wayne, Michigan.[29]

    Laura married **Edmund Christian von der Heide**[26] (b. 22 Dec 1861, d. 25 Jun 1943) on 28 Jun 1899 in Detroit, Wayne, Michigan.[30]

3   iii. **Oscar Christian Weidemann** was born on 1 Aug 1871 in Detroit, Wayne, Michigan,[31] died on 9 Feb 1920 in Detroit, Wayne, Michigan,[26] and was buried on 12 Feb 1920 in Woodlawn Cemetery, Detroit, Wayne, Michigan.[4]

    Oscar married **Mary E. Moynahan** (b. 24 Aug 1876, d. 9 Feb 1920) on 19 May 1901 in Buffalo, Erie, New York.[32]

    iv. **Mathilda "Tilly" Weidemann**[26] was born on 16 Dec 1875 in Detroit, Wayne, Michigan[33] and died on 15 Feb 1961 in Detroit, Wayne, Michigan.[34]

    Noted events in her life were:
- Resided: at 44 Croghan (Monroe), 1880, Detroit, Wayne, Michigan.[12]

- Occupation: teacher and leader in the Detroit school system, 1894-1945.[35]

- Diploma: teaching diploma from Detroit Normal Training School, 1895, Detroit, Wayne, Michigan.[36]

- Occupation: teacher at Everett High School, residing at 116 Monroe, 1895, Detroit, Wayne, Michigan.[37]

- Occupation: teacher residing at 116 Monroe, 1897, Detroit, Wayne, Michigan.[37]

- Occupation: teacher residing at 116 Monroe, 1900, Detroit, Wayne, Michigan.[38]

- Occupation: teacher at Washington Normal School, living at 116 Monroe, 1903-1904, Detroit, Wayne, Michigan.[37] Washington Normal School was a teachers training school that later became Wayne State University College of Education. The school was located on Beaubien and St. Harriet between 1895 and 1914, when it moved to Northwestern High on West Grand.

- Occupation: teacher at Washington Normal School residing at 93 Erskine, 1909, Detroit, Wayne, Michigan.[37]

- Occupation: teacher in the public schools, residing at 93 Erskine St, 1910, Detroit, Wayne, Michigan.[16]

- Occupation: teacher at Washington Normal School, 1911, Detroit, Wayne, Michigan.[37]

- Occupation: assistant principal at Washington Normal School, 1912, Detroit, Wayne, Michigan.[37]

- Graduation: University Of Michigan, 1916, Ann Arbor, Washtenaw, Michigan.[39]

- Occupation: principal Wilkins School, 1916, Detroit, Wayne, Michigan.[40]

- Occupation: principal of Hancock School, 1920-1925, Detroit, Wayne,

Michigan.[41]

- Event: 1930.[42] Delivered an address, "The Winnetka Plan," about pedagogy based on John Dewey's educational philosophy, to the Michigan Education Association.

- Occupation: principal at Chandler Elementary School, 1930-1945, Detroit, Wayne, Michigan.[43]

- Resided: 269 Erskine Street, 1930, Detroit, Wayne, Michigan.[44]

- Event: Letter to editor in Nature Magazine, 1941.[45]

  Dear Sir: I am delighted to find a song in the June issue of Nature Magazine. We shall teach it to the children. Such a song develops the right feeling toward one of God's living creatures. If children had more training along this line, perhaps, as adults, they would never wantonly kill defenseless creatures. I shall be glad to see this new feature continued long enough to give it a fair trial. MATHILDE WEIDEMANN Detroit, Mich.

- Event: 1942.[46] Donated books and filed a report with the Detroit Library titled "One hundred thirty four German classics from the library of the late Christian H. J. Weidemann."

v. **Alma Weidemann**[26] was born on 1 Oct 1876 in Detroit, Wayne, Michigan[47] and died on 4 Jan 1928 in Detroit, Wayne, Michigan.[26]

   Noted events in her life were:
   - Resided: at 44 Croghan (Monroe), 1880, Detroit, Wayne, Michigan.[12]

   - Occupation: milliner residing at 116 Monroe Ave., 1897, Detroit, Wayne, Michigan.[37]

   - Resided: at 116 Monroe Ave., 1900, Detroit, Wayne, Michigan.[14]

   - Visited: Aug 1905, Muskoka, Ontario, Canada.[48]

   - Occupation: saleslady in department store, residing at 93 Erskine, 1910, Detroit, Wayne, Michigan.[16]

   - Fact: 9 Feb 1920.[49] She became Alma Marie Weidemann's guardian when she was orphaned

vi. **Sarah Weidemann** was born on 3 Jul 1878 in Detroit, Wayne, Michigan.[50]

   Research Notes: Sarah does not appear in the 1880 census, but her sister Carrie is listed as 2 years old. Carrie was born in July 1880 but the census was taken in June. It is possible that the wrong name was given for Sarah to the census taker in 1880.

   Noted events in her life were:
   - Resided: 1880, Detroit, Wayne, Michigan.[12]

vii. **Caroline "Carrie" Weidemann** was born on 23 Jul 1880 in Detroit, Wayne, Michigan[51] and died on 29 Nov 1962.[26]

   Noted events in her life were:
   - Resided: at 44 Croghan (Monroe), 1880, Detroit, Wayne, Michigan.[12]

- Occupation: type writer residing at 116 Monroe, 1900, Detroit, Wayne, Michigan.[14]

- Occupation: stenographer and typewriter, Elysian Manufacturing Co. (perfumes and oils), 5 Feb 1901, Detroit, Wayne, Michigan.[52]

- Occupation: stenographer at Detroit and Toledo Shore Line Rail Road residing at 116 Monroe Ave., 5 Feb 1901, Detroit, Wayne, Michigan.[37]

- Occupation: stenographer at Wabash Rail Road residing at 116 Monroe, 1904, Detroit, Wayne, Michigan.[37]

- Occupation: stenographer at the Wabash Rail Road Company residing at 116 Monroe, 1905, Detroit, Wayne, Michigan.[53]

- Visited: Aug 1905, Muskoka, Ontario, Canada.[48]

- Occupation: stenographer at a tobacco company residing at 93 Erskine, 1910, Detroit, Wayne, Michigan.[16]

- Occupation: stenographer at Federal Motor Truck Company residing at 93 Erskine, 1915, Detroit, Wayne, Michigan.[53]

- Occupation: stenographer at a boiler company residing on Erskine, 1930, Detroit, Wayne, Michigan.[44]

Caroline married **George Johannes Dingeldey**,[54] son of **Johann Phillipp Dingeldey** and **Mary Hasselbach,** on 25 Jan 1936.[26] George was born on 28 May 1862 in Buffalo, Erie, New York,[55] died on 24 Dec 1939 in Wayne, Wayne, Michigan,[55] and was buried in Canton, Wayne, Michigan.[56]

Marriage Notes: George Dingeldey's first wife, Mary, was Caroline Weidemann's first cousin.

Noted events in his life were:
- Resided: 1865, Wales, Erie, New York.[57]

- Owned Land: 1905, Canton, Wayne, Michigan.[58]

- Occupation: general farmer, 1910, Canton, Wayne, Michigan.[16]

- Resided: 316 N. Grove, 1916-1935, Ypsilanti, Washtenaw, Michigan.[37]

- Resided: 1920, Ypsilanti, Washtenaw, Michigan.[24]

- Occupation: landlord of rental property, 1930, Ypsilanti, Washtenaw, Michigan.[44]

viii. **Emma Weidemann**[26] was born on 12 Jan 1883 in Detroit, Wayne, Michigan[59] and died on 27 Jul 1964.[26]

Research Notes: A teacher. Sometime after 1930 she was sent to a Canadian facility for treatment of a mental health condition.

Noted events in her life were:
- Resided: at 116 Monroe, 1900, Detroit, Wayne, Michigan.[14]

- Graduated: Michigan State Normal College (now Eastern Michigan University), 1910, Ypsilanti, Washtenaw, Michigan.[60]

- Residing: 1910, Detroit, Wayne, Michigan.[16] Listed on supplemental census sheet.

- Occupation: teacher residing at 93 Erskine, 1915, Detroit, Wayne, Michigan.[37]

- Occupation: teacher living at 93 Erskine Street, 1920, Detroit, Wayne, Michigan.[24]

- Occupation: teacher in the public schools residing at Erskine Street, 1930, Detroit, Wayne, Michigan.[44]

- Resided: Homewood Sanitarium, center for treatment of mental illness and substance abuse, 1953, Quelph, Ontario, Canada.[61]

ix. **Walter Weidemann**[62] was born on 23 Jul 1885 in Detroit, Wayne, Michigan,[63] was christened on 24 Apr 1886 in Wayne, Michigan,[64] died on 2 Jun 1955 in Port Huron, St. Clair, Michigan,[65] and was buried in Woodlawn Cemetery, Detroit, Wayne, Michigan.

Noted events in his life were:
- Resided: 116 Monroe, 1900, Detroit, Wayne, Michigan.[14]

- Occupation: automobile works machinist apprentice living at 93 Erskine, 1910, Detroit, Wayne, Michigan.[16]

- Occupation: engineer residing at 203 Tennyson, 1916, Detroit, Wayne, Michigan.[37]

- Military: registered for WW I draft, 12 Sep 1918, Highland Park, Wayne, Michigan.[66] He was listed as medium height, medium build, brown hair, brown eyes.

- Occupation: machinist at Ford, living at 203 Tennyson, 1918, Highland Park, Wayne, Michigan.[66]

- Occupation: marine engineer residing at 203 Tennyson, 1920, Highland Park, Wayne, Michigan.[24]

- Occupation: exp. engineer at auto factory residing at 203 Tennyson, 1930, Highland Park, Wayne, Michigan.[44]

- Vacation: Hotel Royal Palm, 23 Feb 1931, Pinellas Park, Pinellas, Florida.[67]

- Event: Kidnapped and held in trunk of car, 8 Feb 1936, Detroit, Wayne, Michigan.[68]

- Newspaper Article: from The Detroit Free Press, 9 Feb 1936, Detroit, Wayne, Michigan.[69]

Driver Describes Being 'Kidnaped'
How he was held up, kidnaped and held for seven hours by two men who in the meantime attempted to rob a truck driver was told to Highland Park Police Saturday by Walter Weideman, of 203 Tenny son Ave., Highland Park. The men forced their way into his car when he stopped for a traffic light about 2 p. m., gagged and tied him, and stuffed him into the rear compartment of his coupe, he said. They did not rob him, he said. When the car stopped in front of 85 Englewood Ave. he managed to free himself and crawled out, he told detectives. In the meantime Gordon Chandler, of 10403 Evanston Ave., driver for the Stroh Brewery, reported to police that he had frustrated the attempt of two men to rob him at McNichols Road and Hull Ave. They drove away in a coupe bearing the license number issued to Weideman, police said after a checkup. Highland Park

Police said that the "kidnaping" was the second reported in the last month.

• Newspaper Article: from The Detroit Free Press, 10 Feb 1936, Detroit, Wayne, Michigan.[70]

Captive of Bandits Spends Six Hours in Auto Trunk

The kidnappers who drove for several hours with their victim bound and locked in the rear luggage compartment of his car were sought Sunday by Detroit and Highland Park Police.

The victim, Walter Weideman, of 203 Tennyson Ave., reported that the bandits, both of them armed, forced their way into his coupe after he had parked it on Woodward Ave., near Davison Ave., late Saturday, and drove him to Englewood and Woodward Aves., where one of the bandits got out and entered a vacant building.

The bandit returned with a sawed-off shotgun which he placed on the shelf in back of them in the car, and the journey was resumed. At the Ten Mile Road west of Woodward Ave., he said, the bandits forced him from the car and bound his hands and feet with rope they had purchased at a store en route. Then they shoved him into the compartment and drove for almost six hours, he related.

The car stopped several times, Weideman said, and from the complaint of Gordon Chandler, of 10403 Evanston Ave., a brewery truck driver, one of the stops was occasioned by their attempt to hold him up at McNichols Road and Hull Ave.

Chandler frustrated the holdup, he reported, and obtained the license number of the bandit car, which proved to be the license issued to Weideman, who, police believe, was concealed and locked in the rear compartment at the time of the holdup attempt.

Around 8 p. m., Weideman related, the bandits stopped the car, got out and opened the compartment. They cut Weideman's bonds with a knife and told him to keep quiet for five minutes. After they had gone, Weideman freed himself, found that he was in front of 79 Englewood Ave. and telephoned police from a house at 85 Englewood Ave. Then he went home to tell his wife of his experience in the six hours since he had left her at the Humber Building, 13505 Woodward Ave.

Weideman described the bandits as being between 35 and 40 years old and both dressed in dark hats and blue chinchilla overcoats. One of the kidnapers wore gray gloves and a maroon-colored necktie and had three gold teeth in the upper jaw. The other, of darker complexion, wore a blue-and-white muffler and spats, Weideman observed.

The bandits did not rob him, he said, because be told them that he had only a dollar.

• Occupation: machinist and tool maker in the auto industry residing at 12814 Carn, 1940, Detroit, Wayne, Michigan.[71]

• Military: WW2 draft registration, 1942, Detroit, Wayne, Michigan.[72]

Walter married **Laura Lichtenberg**,[26] daughter of **Christian J. Lichtenberg**[74] and **Caroline Wenzel**,[75] on 1 Jul 1914 in Detroit, Wayne, Michigan.[73] Laura was born on 6 Nov 1878 in Detroit, Wayne, Michigan[76] and died on 24 Oct 1947 in Detroit, Wayne, Michigan.[29]

Weidemann/Wolf

Noted events in her life were:

• Resided: 1900, Detroit, Wayne, Michigan.[14]

• Occupation: clerk at Hudson Motor Car Co. living at 379 Belvidere, 1911, Detroit, Wayne, Michigan.[37]

• Resided: 1920, Detroit, Wayne, Michigan.[24]

• Resided: 1930, Highland Park, Wayne, Michigan.[44]

• Resided: 1940, Highland Park, Wayne, Michigan.[71]

Walter next married **Clara Margaret Diem,** daughter of **Theobald Diem**[14] and **Mary Ann Krantz,**[78] on 4 Jan 1950 in St. Margaret Mary's Church, Detroit, Wayne, Michigan.[77] Clara was born on 24 May 1890 in Carsonville, Sanilac, Michigan,[79] died in Mar 1966 in Port Huron, St. Clair, Michigan,[80] and was buried in Woodlawn Cemetery, Detroit, Wayne, Michigan.

Noted events in her life were:

• Resided: 1900, Washington, Sanilac, Michigan.[14]

• Resided: 1910, Washington, Sanilac, Michigan.[16]

• Occupation: dressmaker, 1920, Washington, Sanilac, Michigan.[24]

• Occupation: garmet cutter at clothing shop, 1930, Port Huron, St. Clair, Michigan.[44]

• Resided: 1950, Carsonville, Sanilac, Michigan.[81]

Weidemann/Wolf

Second Generation (Children)

2. Laura F. Weidemann[26] *(Christian Heinrich Johannes [1])* was born on 13 Dec 1869 in Detroit, Wayne, Michigan[28] and died on 21 Dec 1941 in Detroit, Wayne, Michigan.[29]

Noted events in her life were:
- Resided: 1870, Detroit, Wayne, Michigan.[10]
- Resided: at 44 Croghan (Monroe), 1880, Detroit, Wayne, Michigan.[12]
- Occupation: milliner residing at 116 Monroe, 1895, Detroit, Wayne, Michigan.[37]
- Resided: 356 Fort St., 1900, Detroit, Wayne, Michigan.[14]
- Resided: 920 Meldrum, 1910, Detroit, Wayne, Michigan.[16]
- Resided: 210 Pingree Ave., 1920, Detroit, Wayne, Michigan.[24]
- Resided: 858 Pingree Ave., 1930, Detroit, Wayne, Michigan.[44]
- Resided: 858 Pingree, 1940, Detroit, Wayne, Michigan.[82]

Laura married **Edmund Christian von der Heide**,[26] son of **Christian von der Heide**[83] and **Wilhelmina Backhaus**,[83] on 28 Jun 1899 in Detroit, Wayne, Michigan.[30] Edmund was born on 22 Dec 1861 in Detroit, Wayne, Michigan[84] and died on 25 Jun 1943 in Eloise, Wayne, Michigan.[29]

Noted events in his life were:
- Occupation: bookkeeper residing at 356 Fort St., 1900, Detroit, Wayne, Michigan.[14]
- Resided: 920 Meldrum, 1910, Detroit, Wayne, Michigan.[16]
- Resided: 210 Pingree Ave., 1920, Detroit, Wayne, Michigan.[24]
- Occupation: accountant at wholesale coal company living at 858 Pingree Ave., 1930, Detroit, Wayne, Michigan.[44]
- Resided: 858 Pingree, 1840, Detroit, Wayne, Michigan.[82]

Children from this marriage were:

i. **Elmore Christian von der Heide** was born on 21 Sep 1901 in Detroit, Wayne, Michigan[85] and died on 4 Dec 1983 in St. Clair Shores, Macomb, Michigan.[86]

Noted events in his life were:
- Occupation: physician, 1940, Detroit, Wayne, Michigan.[71]

Elmore married **Vera Archer** about 1929. Vera was born on 8 Feb 1901 in Michigan[87] and died on 8 Apr 1983 in St. Clair Shores, Macomb, Michigan.[86]

Noted events in her life were:
- Occupation: teacher, 1940, Detroit, Wayne, Michigan.[71]

ii. **Carl von der Heide** was born on 5 Jan 1906 in Detroit, Wayne, Michigan[85] and died on 16 Dec 1971 in Royal Oak, Oakland, Michigan.[85]

Weidemann/Wolf

Noted events in his life were:
- Occupation: drugstore salesman, 1930, Detroit, Wayne, Michigan.[44]
- Occupation: salesman, 1940, Detroit, Wayne, Michigan.[71] He is living with his parents, and is married, but his wife and child are not with him.

Carl married **Lillian St. John Morgan** in 1935 in Pittsburgh, Allegheny, Pennsylvania.[88] Lillian was born in 1915 in Pennsylvania.[71]

Noted events in her life were:
- Resided: 1930, Pittsburgh, Allegheny, Pennsylvania.[44]
- Resided: 1940, Wilkinsburg, Allegheny, Pennsylvania.[71] Living with her brother and her daughter, Virginia. She is working as a store clerk.

Carl next married **Ruby Schaper,** daughter of **Frederick Charles Schaper**[90] and **Jennie Smytherman**,[89] on 24 Jan 1942 in Detroit, Wayne, Michigan.[89] Ruby was born about 1912 in Michigan.[44]

Research Notes: She may also be known as Ruby Vinson Johns.

iii. **Virginia Elizabeth von der Heide** was born on 25 Jul 1907 in Detroit, Wayne, Michigan,[91] died on 16 May 1995 in Santa Clara, California,[91] and was buried in Franklin, Oakland, Michigan.[56]

Virginia married **Harry M. Grinnell**. Harry was born on 12 Apr 1903 in New York,[85] died on 9 Jun 1976 in Michigan,[85] and was buried in Franklin, Oakland, Michigan.[56]

Noted events in his life were:
- Occupation: tobacco salesman, 1940, Detroit, Wayne, Michigan.[71]

3. Oscar Christian Weidemann *(Christian Heinrich Johannes [1])* was born on 1 Aug 1871 in Detroit, Wayne, Michigan,[31] died on 9 Feb 1920 in Detroit, Wayne, Michigan,[26] and was buried on 12 Feb 1920 in Woodlawn Cemetery, Detroit, Wayne, Michigan.[4]

General Notes: Oscar grew up in Detroit. He studied art in New York and won a scholarship for a year at the Royal Academy of Art in Berlin. He started a decorating business in Erie, Pennsylvania about 1901. He and his wife moved to Detroit about 1905 where he worked with his father as a painter.

Noted events in his life were:
- Resided: at 44 Croghan (Monroe), 1880, Detroit, Wayne, Michigan.[12]
- Education: completed 8th grade at Washington School (Detroit Public Schools), 24 Jun 1887, Detroit, Wayne, Michigan.[92] Admitted to Detroit High School.
- Education: studying art, about 1891-1893, New York.[93]
- Occupation: painter living with his father, 1891, Detroit, Wayne, Michigan.[94]
- Event: applied for a passport, 10 Oct 1893, New York, New York, New York.[95]
- Arrival: about Nov 1893, Hamburg.[96]
- Arrival: from Hamberg, 6 Nov 1893, Berlin, Germany.[96]

- Education: attended Königliche Kunstschule zu Berlin (Royal Art School in Berlin), about 11 Nov 1893-Nov 1894, Berlin, Germany.[97] Now part of the University of the Arts Berlin.

- Travel: travels to several cities, Jun 1894-Aug 1894, Germany.[96]

- Travel: visits his father's hometown, 6 Aug 1894 to 8 Aug 1894, Neustadt, Schleswig-Holstein, Germany.[96] His sketch of a home at Waschgraben 27 may indicate that his father or a relative lived there.

- Newspaper Article: Detroit Free Press, 30 Sep 1894.[97]

  Among the seventy-nine pupils who attended the Royal School of Art at Berlin during the last semester, nineteen passed the examination. Oscar C. Weidemann of Detroit was one of these, and was also awarded a premium. After studying several years in New York, Mr. Weidemann went to Europe, where he intends to complete his art studies.

- Departure: 17 Feb 1895, Hamburg.[98] on the *SS Russia*

- Arrival: 4 Mar 1895, New York, New York, New York.[9] from Hamburg on the *SS Russia* after a year abroad studying art.

- Residence: 141 W 13th street next door to Anna Sullivan (godmother of his child), before 1900-1901, Erie, Erie, Pennsylvania.[99]

- Residence: 1016 W. 6th (home), 710 State (office in 1903), 1902-1904, Erie, Erie, Pennsylvania.[100]

- Occupation: decorator residing at 1394 Belvidere, 1910, Detroit, Wayne, Michigan.[16]

- Occupation: painter residing at 1394 Belvidere, 1915, Detroit, Wayne, Michigan.[37]

- Occupation: painter in a paint shop residing at at 1394 Belvidere, 1920, Detroit, Wayne, Michigan.[24]

- Cause of death: from The Detroit News, 9 Feb 1920, Detroit, Wayne, Michigan.[101]

  Girl Hears Shots Finds Dying Parents

  Oscar Weidemann, 1294 Belvidere avenue, shot his wife Mary and then turned his revolver on himself, Sunday night, inflicting the wounds of which both died early today at Receiving Hospital. Their daughter, 17 years old, heard the shots and running from a bedroom saw their bodies lying on the floor. She rushed screaming to neighbors, who notified police.

  Weidemann is believed to have been demented. He left a letter accusing his wife, his mother, his relatives and neighbors generally, and describing quarrels. The letter said he had been in Receiving Hospital for alcoholism.

  According to Mrs. Eleanor Neville, next door, they heard the two shots and turned out the lights, fearing he might fire through their windows. Neighbors describe Mrs. Weidemann as a charming woman of 38, crippled, so she could seldom leave the house. They said that Weidemann was jealous, never allowing his wife or daughter to associate with neighbors or, even if he could help it, to walk up Gratiot avenue.

Weidemann/Wolf

Weidemann's letter indicated he had furious quarrels with neighbors over rabbits and chickens invading his yard.

The daughter is being cared for by her grandmother, Mrs. Mary Weidemann, who is in serious condition as a result of a fall sustained a week ago.

• Cause of death: from The Detroit Free Press, 10 Feb 1920, Detroit, Wayne, Michigan.[102]

Woman Murdered by Husband who Turns Gun on Himself

Oscar Weideman, dying, Found with Pistol in Hand

A double shooting, in which Mrs. Mary Weideman, of 1394 Bevidere avenue, was killed by her husband, Oscar, who then turned the weapon on himslf, inflicting what is believed to be a mortal wound.

According to the story told to the police by Alma Weideman, daughter of the principals in the shooting affair, she had gone to bed and her mother was following her, when she heard something on the stairway outside her room. She hurried out and found her mother on the floor at the foot of the steps. He father lay a short distance away, clasping a pistol in his hand. Both were shot though the head. When the police arrived they found another pistol in Weideman's top pocket.

Believed to be Demented

The pair were taken to the Receiving hospital where Mrs. Weideman died at an early hour this morning. Mr. Weideman was not expected to live.

Police believe that Weideman was demented. He is said to have undergone treatment some years ago for mental trouble.

• Memoriam: Sep 1922.[103] $50 donation made in his honor to *The Painter and Decorator* journal.

Oscar married **Mary E. Moynahan,** daughter of **John Minahan**[32] and **Mary O'Brien**,[32] on 19 May 1901 in Buffalo, Erie, New York.[32] Mary was born on 24 Aug 1876 in New York,[104] died on 9 Feb 1920 in Detroit, Wayne, Michigan,[105] and was buried on 12 Feb 1920 in Woodlawn Cemetery, Detroit, Wayne, Michigan.[105]

Christening Notes: Ann Sullivan was godmother at baptism.

General Notes:

Mary claims in her marriage license that she was born in New York City, New York, but more likely she was born in nearby Westchester County, New York. She was disabled, perhaps having a club foot.

She is listed as Mary E. Lardner in the 1880 Albany census, in the same home as her widowed father John Moynahan and her siblings. According to the Albany city archives, Mrs. Lardner had only one daughter, Anne, so Mary. E. Larner was Mary E. Moynahan. After her father left Albany, she stayed with the McNamara family.

It is not known how Oscar and Mary first met, but they were married in Buffalo, New York in 1901. After their daughter, Alma, was born in Erie in 1904, they moved to Detroit in 1905 where Oscar worked as a painter with his father.

In 1920, Mary was murdered by her husband.[49]

Noted events in her life were:

• Religion: Roman Catholic.

• Resided: 1880, Albany, Albany, New York.[12]

Weidemann/Wolf

- Resided: with William and Emma McNamara, 1892, Albany, Albany, New York.[106] Mary does not appear with them in the 1900 census.

- Resided: after May 1901, Erie, Erie, Pennsylvania.[32]

- Resided: at 1394 Belvidere, 1910, Detroit, Wayne, Michigan.[16]

- Resided: at 1394 Belvidere, 1920, Detroit, Wayne, Michigan.[24]

- Cause of death: by murder, shot by her husband., 9 Feb 1920, Detroit, Wayne, Michigan.[107]

The child from this marriage was:

i. **Alma Marie Weidemann** was born on 19 Apr 1904 in Erie, Erie, Pennsylvania,[108] was christened on 23 Jul 1904 in St. Andrew's Catholic Church, Erie, Erie, Pennsylvania,[109] died on 26 Aug 2004 in Ann Arbor, Washtenaw, Michigan,[110] and was buried in Woodlawn Cemetery, Detroit, Wayne, Michigan.

Christening Notes: Ann Sullivan was godmother at baptism

General Notes: Alma Marie Weidemann was born in Erie, Pennsylvania. She was baptized in St Andrew's Catholic Church, Erie, Pennsylvania 23 July 1904 as the "child of Oscar Weidemann and Maria E. Monahan." She moved to Detroit with her parents at an early age. Orphaned at age 15 as a result of a murder-suicide, she then lived with her aunt Alma in Detroit. She graduated from Michigan Normal School (now Eastern Michigan University, Ypsilanti, Michigan). She taught physical education in the Detroit Public Schools. She married Ewald Swanson in 1928. She worked for the state of Michigan in the 1960s and 1970s as a visual and hearing screener in the public schools. She lived in Vassar, Michigan until 2001.

Noted events in her life were:
- Resided: 1910, Detroit, Wayne, Michigan.[16]

- Residence: with her aunt Alma Weidemann, 1920-1923, Detroit, Wayne, Michigan.[111]

- Orphaned: 9 Feb 1920, Detroit, Wayne, Michigan.[112]

- Graduation: Michigan State Normal School (Eastern Michigan University), about 1926, Ypsilanti, Washtenaw, Michigan.

- Occupation: a physical education teacher at Webster School, 1928, Detroit, Wayne, Michigan.[113]

- Resided: 1930, Detroit, Wayne, Michigan.[44]

- Resided: 1935-1993, Vassar, Tuscola, Michigan.[114]

- Obituary: Vassar Pioneer Times, Sep 2004, Vassar, Tuscola, Michigan.[115]

  Alma Swanson of Ann Arbor, and formerly of Vassar, died on Thursday, August 26, 2004, in Ann Arbor. She was 100 years of age. She was born in Erie, Pennsylvania, the daughter of Oscar and Mary (Moynihan) Weidemann. Her husband, Dr. E. C. Swanson, preceded her in death.

  Mrs. Swanson is survived by three children, Shirley Smith, of St. Charles, Illinois, Richard (Jo) Swanson of Newland, North Carolina, and Margery (Jay) Haite of Ann Arbor; nine grandchildren; and seven great grandchildren.

  A family burial will take place in Detroit at Woodlawn Cemetery.

  Those planning an expression of sympathy may wish to consider the Bullard Sanford Memorial Library of Vassar or a memorial of choice.

Weidemann/Wolf

- Obituary: Vassar Pioneer Times, as a letter to the editor by Buck Service, Sep 2004.

Another era in Vassar history has just passed. Mrs. Alma Swanson at 100 years of age has gone to her heavenly reward.

For decades the Swanson family set a standard for the people of Vassar and Mrs. Swanson was quietly elegant. In all the years I have known her, she was always calm and unflappable.

She raised her three children, Shirley, Richard and Margie to remain quiet, studious, and ambitious. The only member of the family that was beyond her control was her husband, "Doc" E.C. Swanson. He was as outgoing as she was quiet.

Mrs. Swanson even bore a striking resemblance to the movie star Gloria Swanson, although there was never an actual connection between the two women.

In recent years she lived alone at her home on North Main Street in Vassar and only moved in with her daughter Shirley when she was no longer able to drive. More recently she moved in with her daughter, Margie, in Ann Arbor, and it was there she spent her last days.

Although gone, her memory still lives in the minds of all who knew her. She was perhaps the last of the old guard in Vassar. The changing of the century and the millennium signalled a time for the slow change of a new society. Will we have a new Alma Swanson to help us set our sights high? She was a grand lady the likes of which we will never see again.

Alma married **Ewald Conrad Swanson M. D.,** son of **Mickel Mickelsson Svens**[116] and **Clara Fredrika Spångberg,** on 22 Jan 1928 in Detroit, Wayne, Michigan. Ewald was born on 3 Jan 1900 in Au Train, Alger, Michigan,[117] died on 26 Sep 1987 in Saginaw, Saginaw, Michigan,[117] and was buried in Woodlawn Cemetery, Detroit, Wayne, Michigan. Another name for Ewald was Dib Swanson.

General Notes: Dr. Ewald C. Swanson graduated from Alma College in central Michigan in 1923 and worked as a woodworker for Ford Motor Co. in Detroit. After working in the medical department at Ford he entered Wayne State University College of Medicine. He interned at Receiving Hospital, Detroit, and became house physician at Wyandotte General Hospital. In 1932 he moved to Vassar, Michigan, and took over the practice of Dr. W. A. Wellmeyer. He was executive secretary of the Michigan State Medical Society. He maintained a summer home in Greenbush, Michigan, on Lake Huron.

Noted events in his life were:
- Resided: 1900, Au Train, Alger, Michigan.[14]

- Resided: 1910, McMillan, Luce, Michigan.[16]

- Graduation: Newberry High School, 1918, Newberry, Luce, Michigan.

- Occupation: die repairman at auto factory, 1920, Detroit, Wayne, Michigan.[44]

Weidemann/Wolf

- Occupation: medic in an automobile factory, 1924, Detroit, Wayne, Michigan.

- Graduation: Alma College, 1923, Alma, Gratiot, Michigan.

- Resided: 1930, Detroit, Wayne, Michigan.[44]

- Occupation: medical attendant at auto plant, 1930, Detroit, Wayne, Michigan.[44]

- Graduation: Wayne State University Medical School, 1931, Detroit, Wayne, Michigan.[118]

- Occupation: physician, 1932, Vassar, Tuscola, Michigan.

- Property: summer cottage, after 1940, Greenbush, Alcona, Michigan.

- Event: visited by August Spangberg, 1955, Newberry, Luce, Michigan.[119]
  August Spångberg, Swedish member of parliament, visited his relatives in Newberry. Ewald took time off from his medical practice to escort August on his trip. Ewald was August's first cousin.

- Organizations: Executive Secretary of the Michigan State Board of Registration, between 1956 and 1967.

- Elected: President of the Federation of State Medical Boards of the United States, 1963.

- Fact: Y-DNA test. Ewald's Y-DNA (via a test of Michael Swanson) shows his patrilineal ancestors were in haplotype N1c1. Approximately 60% of all Finns are in this haplogroup, and its earliest ancestors originated in Southern Siberia circa 10,000 years ago and migrated to Finland circa 5000 years ago.

Wolf/Hillmann in America

First Generation

4. Johann Carl Friedrich Theodor "Carl" Wolf, son of **Carl Friedrich Wolf**[120] and **Christina Dorothea Elisabeth Teage**,[121] was born on 7 Dec 1814 in Zwiedorf, Röckwitz, Mecklenburg-Schwerin,[122] was christened on 11 Dec 1814 in Röckwitz, Mecklenburg-Schwerin,[123] died on 20 Mar 1906 in Michigan City, LaPorte, Indiana,[124] and was buried in Greenwood Cemetery, Michigan City, LaPorte, Indiana.[56] Other names for Johann were Carl Wolff, Charles Wolff, and Karl Wolff.

Christening Notes: Sponsors were Anna Dorothea Friederica, wife of farmer Drews; Johann Friedrich Peters, farmhand in Zwiedorf; Carl Koepke, daylaborer in Zwiedorf.

General Notes: His last address before emigrating was Wildberg, Pomerania. He was educated to the age of fourteen, then apprenticed as a weaver. He brought his wife and eight children to America in 1858 on the sailing ship named *Donau* on a voyage that lasted five weeks. They immigrated through New York, New York and bought a tract of uncleared land fourteen miles west of Detroit where they built a log cabin. After farming the land for several years, they moved to the southwestern corner of Michigan in Berrien County where he bought an eighty acre farm in New Buffalo Township.[125]

Noted events in his life were:
- Confirmation: Lutheran church, 1829, Schossow, Altenhagen, Pommern, Preußen.[126]

- Occupation: weaver, 1841, Wolkow, Wildberg, Pommern, Preußen.[127]

- Occupation: weaver, 1844, Fouquettin, Wildberg, Pommern, Preußen.[127]

- Occupation: weaver, 1858, Wildberg, Wildberg, Pommern, Preußen.[9]

- Emigration: on the Donau, 1 May 1858, Hamburg.[23]

- Immigration: on the ship Donau, 7 Jun 1858, New York, New York, New York.[9]

- Warranty Deed Land: purchased 50 acres, 13 Jan 1859, Nankin, Wayne, Michigan.[128] Purchased land from Murenus Harrison and wife Augusta A. to Carl Wolf and John Conrad, recorded May 5 1860, for $1000 in section 24, Nankin. (The former farm is now a subdivision, and lies on the northeast corner of Middle Belt Road and Avondale Street.)

- Occupation: farmer, 1860, Nankin, Wayne, Michigan.[129]

- Mortgage Cancelled: 3 Aug 1863, Nankin, Wayne, Michigan.[128] The mortgage from Carl Wolff and John Conrad to Marenus Harrison, to Emily Harrison, to Joseph Dittmar, cancelled on face 3 Aug 1863 $200, section 24, Nankin.

- Warranty Deed Land: sold property, 11 Nov 1865, Nankin, Wayne, Michigan.[128] Land transferred from Carl Wolff, Elizabeth Wolff, and John Conrad to Charles Berrosnets (Bewernitz), $2000, section 24, Nankin.

- Occupation: farmer, 1870, New Buffalo, Berrien, Michigan.[10]

- Occupation: farmer, 1880, New Buffalo, Berrien, Michigan.[12]

- Farm: section 20, 80 acres, value $1580, 1892, New Buffalo, Berrien, Michigan.[130]

- Occupation: farmer, 1900, New Buffalo, Berrien, Michigan.[14]

Wolf/Hillmann

- Obituary: Michigan City Dispatch, 22 Mar 1906.[131]

  Karl Wolff died Tuesday at the home of his stepson, John Conrad, 312 East Seventh street, of paralysis. Mr. Wolff was stricken Monday morning, losing his voice and eyesight, and was unconscious until his death, which occurred at 10 o'clock Tuesday night.

  Mr. Wolff was born in Prussia December 7, 1813, and was ninety-two years, three months and thirteen days old. In 1856 he came to this country, settling in Detroit, and from Detroit went to Berrien county, Michigan, where he lived on a farm until four years ago, when he retired and moved to Michigan City. He was married in the old country seventy years ago and his wife died here in 1903. Mr. Wolff leaves, besides the stepson at home with whom he died, three sons, two daughters, twenty-five grandchildren, and eleven great grand children. The children are Charles Wolff, Michigan City; Edmund Wolff, Deadwood, S.D., William Wolff, Miles City, Montana; Mrs. Chris Weidemann, Detroit; and Mrs. Peter Averly, Detroit. The funeral will be held at 2 o'clock Friday afternoon from the home of Charles Wolff at 1120 South Pine street, and the services will be conducted by the Rev. J.G. Hoch, pastor of St. John's Church.

Johann married **Johanna Sophia Elisabeth "Elizabeth" Hillmann,** daughter of **Carl Friedrich Christian Hillmann** and **Christine Sophia Westphal,** about 1836.[132] Johanna was born on 31 May 1811 in Galenbeck, Stavenhagen, Mecklenburg-Schwerin,[133] was christened on 3 Jun 1811 in Kastorf, Stavenhagen, Mecklenburg-Schwerin,[134] and died on 16 Dec 1903 in Michigan City, LaPorte, Indiana.[135] Another name for Johanna was Elizabeth Hillman.[136]

> Marriage Notes: The marriage of Carl Wolf and Elisabeth Hillmann was probably in Kastorf, Stavenhagen.
>
> Christening Notes: Sponsors were girl Catharina Friederica Gilow, Elisabeth Dorothea Rhoden, wife of worker Gottschalk, and worker Johann Joachim Matthies, all from Galenbeck.
>
> Noted events in her life were:
> - Emigration: 1 May 1858, Hamburg.[23] on the bark *Donau*
>
> - Resided: 1860, Nankin, Wayne, Michigan.[129]
>
> - Resided: 1870, New Buffalo, Berrien, Michigan.[10]
>
> - Resided: 1880, New Buffalo, Berrien, Michigan.[12]
>
> - Resided: 1900, New Buffalo, Berrien, Michigan.[14]
>
> - Obituary: Michigan Dispatch, 17 Dec 1903.[137]
>
>   ----------
>
>   Mrs. Wolff is survived by the following children: Mrs. Charles Bevernetz; Mrs. Chris Weideman and Mrs. Augusta Abrele, Detroit; John Conrad, a stepson, this city; Charles Wolff, Michigan City; Edmund Wolff, Deadwood, S.D.; William Wolff, Custer County, Montana.
>
>   ----------
>
> - Obituary: Michigan City News, 23 Dec 1903.[138]
>
>   ----------
>
>   Mrs. Elizabeth Wolff, wife of Carl Wolff, died at her home on East Seventh street at 7:30 o'clock Wednesday evening of old age. She was 92 years, 6 months

and 17 days of age and had been sick less than two days. Deceased was a native of Germany, where she was born May 30, 1811. She was married in Germany, where she was bereaved of her husband, __ Conrad. She was later married to Mr. Wolff, the husband who now survives her. Mr. and Mrs. Wolff came to this country in 1858, locating in Detroit. In 1866 the family moved to New Buffalo, where they resided until 1901 -- when Mr. and Mrs. Wolff and a son moved to this city.

Deceased was the mother of Charles Wolff, well-know resident of this city.

Mrs. Wolff is survived by her husband and seven adult children. John Conrad, residing at home; Charles Wolff of this city; Edmund Wolff residing in South Dakota; William Wolff, living in Miles City, Montana; and three married daughters living in Detroit. One daughter preceded the mother to that home beyond.

Funeral Saturday Afternoon at 2 o'clock, from the home of Charles Wolff, 1120 Pine street, Rev. J.G. Hoch officiating.

Children from this marriage were:

5   i. **Carolina "Lena" Wolf** was born on 28 Mar 1839 in Pommern, Preußen,[139] died on 17 Aug 1904 in Canton, Wayne, Michigan,[140] and was buried in Glenwood Cemetery, Wayne, Wayne, Michigan.

Carolina married **Carl Bewernitz** (b. 22 Jun 1826, d. 14 May 1904) about 1857.[112]

6   ii. **Maria Sophia Caroline Christine Wolf** was born on 3 Aug 1841 in Wolkow, Wildberg, Pommern, Preußen,[20] was christened on 12 Sep 1841 in Wolkow, Wildberg, Pommern, Preußen,[21] and died on 14 Mar 1928 in Detroit, Wayne, Michigan.[22]

Maria married **Christian Heinrich Johannes Weidemann**[1] (b. 26 Feb 1837, d. 22 Jun 1913) on 6 Feb 1868 in Detroit, Wayne, Michigan.[19]

(Duplicate Line. See Person 1 on Page 15)

7   iii. **Auguste Friederike Caroline "Augusta" Wolf** was born on 5 Jan 1844 in Fouquettin, Wildberg, Pommern, Preußen,[141] was christened on 28 Jan 1844 in Wildberg, Wildberg, Pommern, Preußen,[142] died on 21 Aug 1934,[56] and was buried in Woodmere Cemetery, Detroit, Wayne, Michigan.[56]

Auguste married **Peter John Eberle** (b. 21 Oct 1833, d. 17 Jul 1887) on 23 Dec 1863 in Detroit, Wayne, Michigan.[143]

    iv. **Friedrich Wilhelm Christian August Wolf** was born on 3 Feb 1846 in Fouquettin, Wildberg, Pommern, Preußen[144] and was christened on 7 Mar 1846 in Wildberg, Wildberg, Pommern, Preußen.[145]

Christening Notes: Sponsors were: 1. Sexton W. Klunder, 2. sexton August Albrecht, 3. mayor Christ. Dreyer, 4. smith Fr. Heise, Kastorf, 5. Theodor Reisner, 6. shepherd wife Maria Schroeder, Kastorf, 7. Maria Müller, wife of colonist Müller.

Noted events in his life were:
• Emigration: on the Donau, 1 May 1858, Hamburg.[23]

8   v. **Carl "Charles" Wolf** was born on 7 Feb 1847 in Pommern, Preußen,[146] died on 11 Jan

1924 in Michigan City, LaPorte, Indiana,[147] and was buried in Greenwood Cemetery, Michigan City, LaPorte, Indiana.

Carl married **Caroline Magdalena Koch** (b. 1855, d. about 1882) on 30 Oct 1877 in Romulus, Wayne, Michigan.[73]

Carl next married **Ida Cook** (b. 9 Dec 1865, d. 11 Mar 1947) on 30 Mar 1884.[112]

9   vi. **Wilhelm Friedrich Adolph "Edmund" Wolf**[148] was born on 26 Dec 1848 in Fouquettin, Wildberg, Pommern, Preußen,[149] was christened on 29 Dec 1848 in Wildberg, Wildberg, Pommern, Preußen,[150] died on 19 May 1934 in Detroit, Wayne, Michigan,[151] and was buried in Grand Lawn Cemetery, Detroit, Wayne, Michigan.

Wilhelm married **Louise Sophie Koch** (b. 27 Jan 1864) on 7 Mar 1882 in Detroit, Wayne, Michigan.[152]

Wilhelm next married **Esther "Et" Maria Bills** (b. 25 Nov 1858, d. 8 Nov 1933) on 9 Jun 1894 in El Reno, Canadian, Oklahoma.[153]

vii. **Wilhelmine Sophie Caroline Dorothea "Emilie" Wolf** was born on 22 May 1852 in Fouquettin, Wildberg, Pommern, Preußen[154] and was christened on 26 Jun 1852 in Wildberg, Wildberg, Pommern, Preußen.[155]

Christening Notes: Sponsors were: 1. Farmer wife Emilie Dreyer, 2. cartwright wife Friederike Hintzpeter, 3. miller wife Marie Dreyer, colonist wife Christine Mueller, farmer Friedrich Kruse, 6. bricklayer Theodor Peter, 7. colonist Christoph Schramm, 8. Carl Reisner.

Noted events in her life were:
- Emigration: on the Donau, 1 May 1858, Hamburg.[23]
- Resided: 1860, Nankin, Wayne, Michigan.[129]

10   viii. **Johann Carl Friedrich Wilhelm "William Wallace" Wolf** was born on 19 Jul 1855 in Fouquettin, Wildberg, Pommern, Preußen,[156] was christened on 30 Jul 1855 in Wildberg, Wildberg, Pommern, Preußen,[157] died on 9 Mar 1934 in Miles City, Custer, Montana,[158] and was buried in Custer County Cemetery, Miles City, Custer, Montana.[56]

Johann married **Lucille Perry** (b. 27 Oct 1864, d. 30 May 1951) on 17 Feb 1892 in Mount Clemens, Macomb, Michigan.[159]

Johann next married **Rose Elizabeth Shannon**[160] (b. 19 Oct 1886, d. 24 Nov 1966) on 7 Dec 1929 in Big Timber, Sweet Grass, Montana.[161]

Wolf/Hillmann

Second Generation (Children)

5. Carolina "Lena" Wolf *(Johann Carl Friedrich Theodor "Carl"* [1]*)* was born on 28 Mar 1839 in Pommern, Preußen,[139] died on 17 Aug 1904 in Canton, Wayne, Michigan,[140] and was buried in Glenwood Cemetery, Wayne, Wayne, Michigan. Another name for Carolina was Carolena Wolff.

> Noted events in her life were:
> * Residence: 1860, Nankin, Wayne, Michigan.[129]
> * Occupation: housekeeper, 1904, Canton, Wayne, Michigan.[162]

Carolina married **Carl Bewernitz** about 1857.[112] Carl was born on 22 Jun 1826 in Pommern, Preußen,[163] died on 14 May 1904 in Nankin, Wayne, Michigan,[164] and was buried in Glenwood Cemetery, Wayne, Wayne, Michigan. Other names for Carl were Carl Berrosnets and Charles Bewernitz.

> General Notes: Took over the Wolff farm at Nankin, Michigan when the Wolffs moved west.

> Noted events in his life were:
> * Occupation: farmer, 1860, Nankin, Wayne, Michigan.

Children from this marriage were:

> i. **John Bewernitz** was born in 1857 in Preußen.[129]
>
> ii. **Mary Bewernitz**[56] was born on 22 Apr 1860 in Nankin, Wayne, Michigan,[165] died on 30 Sep 1934 in Ypsilanti, Washtenaw, Michigan,[165] and was buried in Canton, Wayne, Michigan.[56]
>
>> Noted events in her life were:
>> * Resided: 1920, Ypsilanti, Washtenaw, Michigan.[24]
>
> Mary married **George Johannes Dingeldey**,[54] son of **Johann Phillipp Dingeldey** and **Mary Hasselbach**. George was born on 28 May 1862 in Buffalo, Erie, New York,[55] died on 24 Dec 1939 in Wayne, Wayne, Michigan,[55] and was buried in Canton, Wayne, Michigan.[56]
>
>> Noted events in his life were:
>> * Resided: 1865, Wales, Erie, New York.[57]
>> * Owned Land: 1905, Canton, Wayne, Michigan.[58]
>> * Occupation: general farmer, 1910, Canton, Wayne, Michigan.[16]
>> * Resided: 316 N. Grove, 1916-1935, Ypsilanti, Washtenaw, Michigan.[37]
>> * Resided: 1920, Ypsilanti, Washtenaw, Michigan.[24]
>> * Occupation: landlord of rental property, 1930, Ypsilanti, Washtenaw, Michigan.[44]
>
> iii. **Charles F. Bewernitz** was born on 22 Jan 1864 in Michigan,[164] died on 14 Apr 1919,[164] and was buried in Glenwood Cemetery, Wayne, Wayne, Michigan.
>
>> Noted events in his life were:
>> * Occupation: farmer, 1910, Nankin, Wayne, Michigan.[16]
>
> Charles married **Alvina Schmidt**,[166] daughter of **Charles Schmidt**[166] and **Sophie Wint**,[166] on 2 Jun 1891 in Taylor, Wayne, Michigan.[166] Alvina was born in 1870 in

Michigan.[73]

iv. **August Christoph Johann Friedrich Bewernitz** was born on 2 Aug 1867 in Nankin, Wayne, Michigan,[167] was christened on 20 Oct 1867 in Dearborn Heights, Wayne, Michigan,[168] died on 22 Feb 1942 in Inkster, Wayne, Michigan,[167] and was buried in Wayne, Wayne, Michigan,.[56]

Noted events in his life were:
- Occupation: farmer, 1930, Inkster, Wayne, Michigan.[44]

- Resided: 1940, Inkster, Wayne, Michigan.[71]

August married **Clara Querfeld**,[73] daughter of **Morris Querfeld**[73] and **Lena Vought**,[73] on 7 Nov 1894 in Dearborn, Wayne, Michigan.[73] Clara was born on 26 Jan 1869 in Michigan,[164] died on 7 Dec 1901,[164] and was buried in Wayne, Wayne, Michigan.[56]

August next married **Annie Goldner**,[112] daughter of **Charles Goldner**[169] and **Selma H. Fruehauff**,[169] on 21 Jun 1916 in Detroit, Wayne, Michigan.[73] Annie was born on 16 Jun 1877 in Detroit, Wayne, Michigan[16] and died on 18 Jan 1944 in Detroit, Wayne, Michigan.

Noted events in her life were:
- Resided: 1910, Detroit, Wayne, Michigan.[16]

6. Maria Sophia Caroline Christine Wolf (*Johann Carl Friedrich Theodor "Carl"* [1]) was born on 3 Aug 1841 in Wolkow, Wildberg, Pommern, Preußen,[20] was christened on 12 Sep 1841 in Wolkow, Wildberg, Pommern, Preußen,[21] and died on 14 Mar 1928 in Detroit, Wayne, Michigan.[22] Another name for Maria was Mary Wolff.

Christening Notes: Sponsors were: 1. girl Christine Wolf, Schossow, 2. girl Sophie Wolf, Schossow, 3. girl Henriette Hillmann, Galenbeck, 4. wife Johanna Feul, Galenbeck, 5. Joachim Ehrenreich, Wolde, 6. Johann Sievert, Wolkow, 7. bricklayer Martin Tessin, Japzow.

Noted events in her life were:
- Emigration: 1 May 1858, Hamburg.[23] on the bark *Donau*.

- Immigration: 7 Jun 1858, New York, New York, New York.[9]

- Resided: at 44 Croghan (Monroe), 1880, Detroit, Wayne, Michigan.[12]

- Resided: 116 Monroe, 1900, Detroit, Wayne, Michigan.[14]

- Resided: 93 Erskine, 1910, Detroit, Wayne, Michigan.[16] 7 of 8 children living.

- Resided: 93 Erskine, 1920, Detroit, Wayne, Michigan.[24]

- Fact: Home renumbered from 93 to 269 Erskine, 1921, Detroit, Wayne, Michigan.[25]

Wolf/Hillmann

Maria married **Christian Heinrich Johannes Weidemann**,[1] son of **Claus Friederich Weidemann**[1] and **Anna Catherina Hedewig Ahrend**,[1] on 6 Feb 1868 in Detroit, Wayne, Michigan.[19] Christian was born on 26 Feb 1837 in Neustadt, Ostholstein, Holstein,[2] died on 22 Jun 1913 in Detroit, Wayne, Michigan,[3] and was buried on 25 Jun 1913 in Woodlawn Cemetery, Detroit, Wayne, Michigan.[4] The cause of his death was apoplexy.

> General Notes: Born in Neustadt in Holstein, he lived in Austria before coming to America in 1866 with his brother. He worked for Wright and Company, a nationally-known design firm, which provided interior design and architecture services for large homes, commercial buildings, and government buildings. He worked as a fresco painter and supervised large projects including the interior decoration of the Michigan capitol building.

Noted events in his life were:

- Resided: on Waschgraben, circa 1846, Neustadt, Ostholstein, Holstein.[5] The family probably resided on Waschgraben, which is east of the church in the 3rd quarter. Oscar Weidemann made a sketch of the house when he visited Neustadt in 1894.

- Resided: about 1860, Vienna, Austria.[6]

- Occupation: painter, before 1866, Hamburg.[7]

- Emigration: 15 May 1866, Hamburg.[8] on the bark *Apollo* with his brother Henry

- Immigration: 6 Jul 1866, New York, New York, New York.[9] on the *Apollo*

- Occupation: fresco painter, 1870, Detroit, Wayne, Michigan.[10]

- Occupation: fresco painter, 1877, Detroit, Wayne, Michigan.[11]

- Occupation: fresco painter residing downtown at 44 Croghan (Monroe) near Cadillac Square, 1880, Detroit, Wayne, Michigan.[12]

- Occupation: decorating supervisor with William Wright Co. at the state capitol building, about 1888-1889, Lansing, Ingham, Michigan.[13]

- Occupation: decorator, 1900, Detroit, Wayne, Michigan.[14]

- Home Built: from The Detroit Free Press, 16 Apr 1905, Detroit, Wayne, Michigan.[15]

  Architects Norval Wardrop and Louis Keil have prepared plans and have let contracts for a residence for Christian Weidemann, on the north side of Erskine street, between John R. and Brush streets. It is to be a solid paving brick house, slate root, galvanized cornice, hardwood finish for the interior and hardwood floors in the principal rooms, hot water for heating, combination lighting, mantels and modern sanitary plumbing. The dimensions are 32x50. The following contracts have been awarded: Mason work, LeMay & Whelun; carpenter, George Watt; plumbing and heating, John F. Jones; plastering, Gustay Jahnke; painting, William Wright Co.

- Occupation: master painter, 1910, Detroit, Wayne, Michigan.[16]

- Resided: 93 Erskine, 1913, Detroit, Wayne, Michigan.[17]

- Cause of death: apoplexy, 22 Jun 1913.[4]

- Obituary: from the Detroit Free Press, 23 Jun 1913.[18]

Christian Weidemann, Aged Designer, Dies

Succumbs to Heart Disease Sunday Monday at his Detroit Home.

Christian Weideman, 75 years old, for more than 40 years connected with the firm of William Wright & Co., as a designer, dies suddenly early Sunday morning at his home, 93 Erskine street, of heart disease.

Mr. Weideman was in his usual health when he retired Saturday night but complained about 2:30 a. m. of being ill and later died.

Mr. Weideman, along with work on other public buildings, superintended the decoration of the state capitol at Lansing about 20 years ago.

The funeral will be held Wednesday at 2 p. m. from the house and burial will be private.

Mr. Weideman was born in Neustadt, Germany, in 1837, and came to Detroit about 45 years ago. His first employment in Detroit was with William Wright and he continued with him until his death. As the firm went through various changes in ownership, management and name, Mr. Weideman acquired a financial interest.

He is survived by a widow and seven children, Oscar, Mathilde, assistant principal of the Detroit Normal School, Alma Caroline, Emma, Walter and Mrs. E. Von der Heide.

(Duplicate Line. See Person 1 on Page 15)

7. Auguste Friederike Caroline "Augusta" Wolf *(Johann Carl Friedrich Theodor "Carl"* [1]*)* was born on 5 Jan 1844 in Fouquettin, Wildberg, Pommern, Preußen,[141] was christened on 28 Jan 1844 in Wildberg, Wildberg, Pommern, Preußen,[142] died on 21 Aug 1934,[56] and was buried in Woodmere Cemetery, Detroit, Wayne, Michigan.[56] Other names for Auguste were Fredricka Eberle and Augusta Wolff.

Christening Notes: Sponsors were: 1. Wife of colonist (farmer) Friederike Schramm, 2. girl Auguste Reisner, 3. weaver Christian Mueller.

Noted events in her life were:
- Emigration: on the Donau, 1 May 1858, Hamburg.[23]

- Resided: 1870, Detroit, Wayne, Michigan.[10]

- Resided: 50 Commonwealth Ave. with her son Frederick, 1910, Detroit, Wayne, Michigan.[16]

- Residence: with her children Clara and Fred, 1930, Detroit, Wayne, Michigan.[44]

Auguste married **Peter John Eberle** on 23 Dec 1863 in Detroit, Wayne, Michigan.[143] Peter was born on 21 Oct 1833 in Baden,[170] died on 17 Jul 1887,[56] and was buried in Woodmere Cemetery, Detroit, Wayne, Michigan.

Noted events in his life were:
- Occupation: butcher, 1870, Detroit, Wayne, Michigan.[10]

Wolf/Hillmann

Children from this marriage were:

 i. **Charles T. Eberle** was born on 21 Sep 1865 in Michigan[171] and died on 28 Apr 1953 in Dallas, Dallas, Texas.[172]

  Noted events in his life were:
  • Resided: 1910, Lagow, Dallas, Texas.[16] Living with wife, Della, and children Guy and Charles.

  Charles married **Mary Della Sphar** on 27 Aug 1889 in Buchanan, Missouri.[173] Mary was born on 16 Dec 1866 in Missouri[174] and died on 30 Jan 1952 in Dallas, Dallas, Texas.[175]

 ii. **Martha "Mattie" Eberle** was born on 5 Aug 1867 in Detroit, Wayne, Michigan[176] and died on 5 Nov 1940 in Detroit, Wayne, Michigan.[169]

  Martha married **Elijah E. Patterson,** son of **James William Patterson**[73] and **Phoebe Blackmer**,[73] on 19 Oct 1887 in Detroit, Wayne, Michigan.[73] Elijah was born on 27 Sep 1865 in Detroit, Wayne, Michigan[177] and died on 5 May 1951 in Detroit, Wayne, Michigan.[178]

  Noted events in his life were:
  • Occupation: veterinary saleperson, 1930, Detroit, Wayne, Michigan.[44]

 iii. **Alvira Eberle** was born in 1869 in Michigan.[10]

 iv. **Clara Eberle** was born in 1870,[56] died on 13 Feb 1948,[56] and was buried in Woodmere Cemetery, Detroit, Wayne, Michigan.[56]

  Noted events in her life were:
  • Resided: with her brother, Frederick, and mother, 1930, Detroit, Wayne, Michigan.[44]

 v. **Frederick Eberle** was born on 1 Apr 1873 in Detroit, Wayne, Michigan,[179] died on 12 Oct 1951 in Detroit, Wayne, Michigan,[165] and was buried in Woodmere Cemetery, Detroit, Wayne, Michigan.[56]

  Noted events in his life were:
  • Occupation: salesperson at machinery depot, 1910, Detroit, Wayne, Michigan.[16] Living with his widowed mother.

  • Occupation: owner/manager of Pennisular Machinery Co., 1917, Detroit, Wayne, Michigan.[180]

 vi. **Adolph "Edward" Eberle** was born on 17 Mar 1874 in Detroit, Wayne, Michigan,[64] died on 12 Jul 1892,[56] and was buried in Woodmere Cemetery, Detroit, Wayne, Michigan.[56]

 vii. **Caroline "Lena" Eberle** was born on 31 Jul 1877 in Michigan,[181] died on 29 Apr 1943,[56] and was buried in Litchfield Cemetery, Litchfield, Sherman, Nebraska.[56]

  Noted events in her life were:
  • Resided: 1917, Nebraska.[180]

  • Resided: 1930, Omaha, Douglas, Nebraska.[44]

  Caroline married **Delavan Baldwin Marshall**,[182] son of **Richard S. Marshall**[81] and **Caroline Munson**,[81] on 22 Jun 1904 in Detroit, Wayne, Michigan.[166] Delavan was born on 20 Nov 1877 in Massachusetts,[183] died in Mar 1940,[56] and was buried in Forest Lawn Memorial Park, Omaha, Douglas, Nebraska.[56]

Noted events in his life were:
- Occupation: salesman and local manager, 1930, Omaha, Douglas, Nebraska.[44]

8. Carl "Charles" Wolf (*Johann Carl Friedrich Theodor "Carl"* [1]) was born on 7 Feb 1847 in Pommern, Preußen,[146] died on 11 Jan 1924 in Michigan City, LaPorte, Indiana,[147] and was buried in Greenwood Cemetery, Michigan City, LaPorte, Indiana.

Noted events in his life were:
- Emigration: on the Donau, 1 May 1858, Hamburg.[23]

- Resided: 1860, Nankin, Wayne, Michigan.[129]

- Event: was a freight driver for the army during the Battle of the Little Bighorn (Custer's Last Stand), 25 Jun 1876, Crow Agency, Big Horn, Montana.[125]

- Occupation: farmer, 1877, Michigan City, LaPorte, Indiana.[125]

- Occupation: landlord, 1900, Michigan City, LaPorte, Indiana.[14]

- Occupation: bank director, after 1900.[125]

- Bio: from Indiana and Indianans, 1919.[125]

    Charles Wolff, a real estate man of Michigan City and for many years an active farmer in that vicinity, is one of the few surviving men who can talk intimately of personal experience in the far West when progress of civilization was beset on every hand by the obstacles of nature and the perils of Indian warfare.

    Mr. Wolff was born in Prussia, Germany, in February 1846, but has lived in the United States more than sixty years. His father, Carl Wolff, was also a native of Prussia, where his parents spent all their days. Carl Wolff attended school to the age of fourteen, then served an apprenticeship at the carpenter's [correction: weaver's] trade, and followed it as his occupation in Germany until 1856, when he brought his wife and eight children to America. They made the passage on a sailing vessel named Donau, under Captain Myers, and were five weeks and three days on the ocean. Landing at New York they pushed on westward to Wayne County, Michigan, buying a tract of land fourteen miles west of Detroit. A log cabin and a small cleared space constituted the improvements. The log cabin was the first home of the Wolff family in America. Carl Wolff gave his time to clearing the land and tilling the soil. There was but little demand for either wood or lumber, and great maple logs were rolled together and burned. Some years later the Wolff family moved to the southwestern corner of Michigan in Berrien County, where Carl Wolff bought an eighty acre farm in Buffalo Township. That was his home for twenty-eight years, and he spent his last days in Michigan City, where he died in 1908, at the venerable age of ninety-three. He married Elizabeth Hillman, who died in 1906, aged also ninety-three years. Their children were named Caroline, Ricca, Gustav, Charles, Edmond, Amelia, and William. The mother by a former marriage also had a son, named John Conrad.

    Charles Wolff was ten years old when his parents came to this country. He had attended school in Germany and was also a pupil in a log cabin school in

Wolf/Hillmann

Wayne County, Michigan. At the age of eighteen he left home and began to make his own way in the world. Following the course of the Union Pacific and the Northern Pacific Railroad he eventually arrived in San Francisco, but remained on the Pacific coast only a short time before he returned home, passing through Kansas City, which was then a very small town. He reached Michigan in the spring of 1868, and in April, 1869, was again on his way to the West in the employ of the Northern Pacific Railroad. He went to the Red River of the North at a time when Northern Minnesota and the Dakotas were an almost unexplored territory, having only a few scattered settlements along the stream. In 1870 he preempted a tract of Government land in North Dakota. There was no railroad within miles, and while looking after his land he also used his team and wagon for freighting. In 1873 he had charge of the freight train that went West with General Custer for exploration of the Big Horn Mountain country in Montana. In 1874 he was in the Black Hills expedition. All these expeditions were fraught with many adventures and hardships. At one time Mr. Wolff's wagon train was confronted by a stream about twelve feet wide and eight feet deep, with a rapid current of water. His wagons were loaded with boxes of bacon. He had to solve a practical engineering problem without undue delay, and he ordered his men to unload the bacon and place it in the stream, effecting a temporary dam and bridge over which the teams crossed successfully. The boxes of bacon were then taken up and reloaded without injury to the meat. Mr. Wolff was also with General Custer's freight train in 1876 when Custer was on his last expedition. The general and his troops left the train at midnight, and the following day were beset by the Indians and massacred practically to a man. The freight train had a guard of forty soldiers and started at daylight, but after going about a mile were surrounded by Indians, and a halt was called and the soldiers and drivers dug themselves in and stood a siege, for two weeks before being relieved by General Crook and taken to the Black Hills. Mr. Wolff did not receive his pay from the Government for this service until two years later.

In the meantime he had enough of the perils and adventures of the far West, and returning East he bought a farm in Michigan Township, three miles from Michigan City. He was steadily engaged in its management and tilling until 1900, when he moved to Michigan City and entered the real estate business.

In 1877 Mr. Wolff married Miss Caroline Cook. She was born in Wayne County, Michigan, where her parents, Felix and Elizabeth Cook, natives of Saxony, were early settlers. Mrs. Wolff died in 1884, mother of two children, Ora, now deceased, and Clarissa, wife of George Davis. In 1886 Mr. Wolff married Ida Cook, who was born in Michigan City, a daughter of Charles and Charlotte Cook. They have four children: William C.; Laura, a kindergarten teacher; Arthur; and Alta. The son Arthur was with the American Expeditionary Forces in France.

- Occupation: landlord, 1920, Michigan City, LaPorte, Indiana.[24]

- Naturalization: 8 Mar 1920, Michigan City, LaPorte, Indiana.[184] residing at 1120 Pine St.

- Obituary: from La Porte County News Dispatch, 12 Jan 1924.[185]

     Charles Wolff Died Last Night
     Ill only a week; was fine type of manhood; well thought of on the Community

where he lived

One of Michigan City's best known and most highly respected citizens reached the end of his life well spent at 11:50 o'clock Friday night when Charles Wolff expired at his home, 1120 Pine street. His last illness extended over a period of but one week. His death was attributed to heart trouble.

Mr. Wolff was born on Feb. 7, 1847, in Germany, and came to America when he was nine years of age. The early part of his life was spent in the wester states. He moved on a farm three miles east of Michigan City in 1877 and lived there until 1899 when he moved to Michigan City.

In 1877 he and Caroline Kock, of Detroit, were united in marriage. Three children blessed this union. Mrs. George Shane, formerly Ora L. Wolff, is dead. One of Mr. and Mrs Wolff's children died in infancy. One daughter, Mrs. Clarissa Davis, resides in Chicago. Mrs. Wolff died in 1882. Mr. Wolff was, in 1884, married to Ida Cook, the widow who now survives him. Five children were born to them. One child is dead.

Besides the widow he leaves the following children, by the second marriage: William C. Wolff, Arthur A. Wolff, and Mrs. C. L Stronte, of South Bend. There survive also six grandchildren, two sisters and two brothers.

Mr. Wolff was a member of the St. John's Evangelical church. He was director of the First National bank and Michigan City Trust and Savings bank, he having been re-elected to the directorate to each of these institutions this week. Mr. Wolff was the type of man one could well feel proud to call a friend. Steady and reliable at all times he ever gave a friendly greeting and with the utmost sincerity. In his death the community loses one of its finest men and a home is bereft of a good husband and father. The relatives have the sympathy of a large number of people in their sorrow.

The funeral will be held Monday afternoon with services at 2:30 o'clock in the family home, 1120 Pine street. Rev. Paul Irion, pastor of St. John's Evangelical church, will officiate. Burial in Greenwood cemetery. The body may be viewed at any time Sunday afternoon or evening.

Carl married **Caroline Magdalena Koch,** daughter of **Christian Koch** and **Catherine Lole,**[169] on 30 Oct 1877 in Romulus, Wayne, Michigan.[73] Caroline was born in 1855 in Romulus, Wayne, Michigan[73] and died about 1882.[125]

Children from this marriage were:

     i. **Ora Louise Wolff** was born on 28 Aug 1878,[56] died on 21 Feb 1905,[56] and was buried in Rosehill Cemetery and Mausoleum, Chicago, Cook, Illinois.[56]

     Ora married **M. George Shoen**[56] on 16 Feb 1904 in Chicago, Cook, Illinois.[186]

    ii. **Clarissa Wolff**[187] was born on 4 Feb 1880 in Michigan City, LaPorte, Indiana,[187] died on 2 Jun 1927 in Chicago, Cook, Illinois,[187] and was buried on 6 Jun 1927 in Michigan City, LaPorte, Indiana.[187]

     Noted events in her life were:
     • Occupation: Nurses Registry.[187]

     Clarissa married **George T. Davis**[188] on 22 Sep 1917 in Lake, Indiana.[189]

Carl next married **Ida Cook,** daughter of **Charles Cook** and **Charlotte Westphal,** on 30 Mar 1884.[112] Ida was born on 9 Dec 1865 in Michigan City, LaPorte, Indiana,[187] died on 11 Mar 1947,[56] and was buried in Greenwood Cemetery, Michigan City, LaPorte, Indiana.[56]

Noted events in her life were:
- Resided: 1880, Cool Spring, LaPorte, Indiana.[12]
- Resided: 1900, Michigan City, LaPorte, Indiana.[14]
- Resided: 1910, Michigan City, LaPorte, Indiana.[16]
- Resided: 1920, Michigan City, LaPorte, Indiana.[24]
- Resided: 1930, Michigan City, LaPorte, Indiana.[44]
- Resided: 1940, Mishawaka, St. Joseph, Indiana.[71]

Children from this marriage were:

i. **William Charles Wolff**[190] was born on 17 Apr 1885 in Indiana,[191] died on 20 Oct 1938,[56] and was buried in Greenwood Cemetery, Michigan City, LaPorte, Indiana.[56]

   Noted events in his life were:
   - Occupation: woked at gas station, 1917, Michigan City, LaPorte, Indiana.[180]

   William married **Ethel Frances Deming**,[190] daughter of **Frank Charles Deming**[190] and **Stella Adel Nichols**,[190] on 11 Apr 1913 in LaPorte, Indiana.[190] Ethel was born about 1887 in Indiana,[16] died on 2 May 1933,[56] and was buried in Greenwood Cemetery, Michigan City, LaPorte, Indiana.[56]

ii. **Laura Wolff** was born on 18 Jan 1888 in Indiana,[192] died in Feb 1968,[85] and was buried in Mishawaka, St. Joseph, Indiana.[56]

   Laura married **Charles Leuran Strome**, son of **David Strome**[193] and **Nettie Darling**,.[193] Charles was born on 6 May 1894 in Warsaw, Coshocton, Ohio,[194] died in 1940,[56] and was buried in Mishawaka, St. Joseph, Indiana.[56]

iii. **Arthur Albert Wolff** was born on 5 Nov 1893 in Indiana,[195] died on 2 Dec 1964,[56] and was buried in Michigan City, LaPorte, Indiana.[56]

   Noted events in his life were:
   - Occupation: salesman, 1940, Michigan City, LaPorte, Indiana.[71]

   Arthur married **Florentine M. Kreuger**. Florentine died on 24 Mar 1979[56] and was buried in Greenwood Cemetery, Michigan City, LaPorte, Indiana.[56]

iv. **Alta Marion Wolff**[112] was born on 31 Aug 1900 in Michigan City, LaPorte, Indiana[196] and died on 13 Aug 1994 in Simsbury, Hartford, Connecticut.[197]

   Noted events in her life were:
   - Resided: 1935, Oak Park, Cook, Illinois.[71]
   - Resided: 1940, St. Louis, Missouri.[71]
   - Obituary: from Hartford Currant, 15 Aug 1994.[198]

     GRAY. Alta M. (Wolff) Gray, 93, of Great Pond Road, Simsbury, wife of the late F.A. Gray, died Saturday (August 13, 1994) at McLean Home in Simsbury. She was born August 31, 1900 in Michigan City, Ind., daughter of the late Charles and Ida (Cook) Wolff, and had lived in Des Moines, Iowa prior to moving to West Simsbury 12 years ago. She is survived by a daughter, JoAnn Rees of Simsbury; a son, James Gray of Seattle, Wash.; nine grandchildren; and 11 great- grandchildren. Memorial funeral service will be at McLean Home at the

convenience of the family. Burial will be in Green Wood Cemetery, Michigan City, Ind. There are no calling hours. Vincent Funeral Home, 880 Hopmeadow Street, Simsbury has charge of arrangements.

Alta married **Fayne A. Gray**[112] on 19 May 1920 in St. Joseph, Berrien, Michigan.[199] Fayne was born on 24 May 1901 in Illinois[73] and died in Jan 1982 in Polk, Iowa.[200]

Noted events in his life were:
• Occupation: real estate, 1930, Michigan City, LaPorte, Indiana.[44]

9. Wilhelm Friedrich Adolph "Edmund" Wolf[148] *(Johann Carl Friedrich Theodor "Carl"* [1]*)* was born on 26 Dec 1848 in Fouquettin, Wildberg, Pommern, Preußen,[149] was christened on 29 Dec 1848 in Wildberg, Wildberg, Pommern, Preußen,[150] died on 19 May 1934 in Detroit, Wayne, Michigan,[151] and was buried in Grand Lawn Cemetery, Detroit, Wayne, Michigan. Another name for Wilhelm was Edmund Wolff.

> Christening Notes: Sponsors were: 1. Tailor Ludwig Hansen, 2. weaver Adolph Schmidt, 3. wife Johanna Segebrecht

Noted events in his life were:
• Emigration: on the Donau, 1 May 1858, Hamburg.[23]

• Resided: 1860, Nankin, Wayne, Michigan.[129]

• Early Settler: from Historical Atlas of Dakota (1884), 1876, Crook City, Lawrence, Dakota Territory.[201]

> [Crook City] is one of the oldest places in the northern Hills. It was originally called "Camp Crook", in honor of General Crook, who encamped on the site with a considerable force in 1875. The general also visited the place a second time in 1876.
>
> The town is well situated on the Whitewood Creek, about seven miles by road, northeast of Deadwood at the foot of the Hills where the creek debouches into the open country. It is in a natural basin, having the main Hills on the southwest, and a chain of low hills sweeping around it on the north, east and west.
>
> There was considerable excitement here and a numerous population in 1876, when the placers of Whitewood Creek were believed to be rich in float gold. Among the early comers were the following names persons: William Cable, J. B. Whitson, S. W. Valentine, Christian Speigel, A. L. Burk, D. B. Ross, H. M. Vroman, Mrs. Nellie Gray, William Wigginton, Richard Mills, Richard Stevens, E. R. Collins, W. D. Wakeman, Charles Frances, Major James Whitehead, Benjamin Hazen, Samuel Jackson, J. T. Stewart, Christian Kuhl, Moses Haines, James Herringden, Charles Lawn, Thomas Moore, William Smith, J. and B. Logan, John Gallenger, William Wade, Thomas Shannon, Henry Ash, George Mattocks, Ed. Wolf, Rd. Donahue, J. and N. McMahon, Wiley Winton and James Coyne.
>
> The Indians were very troublesome in 1876-77 and a number of people were killed by them in the vicinity of Crook City, among whom were Rev. Smith, three of the Wagnus family, a Mr. McLaren and others to the number of from eight to ten, who were buried in the Crook City burying ground. Charles Mason, who went out from Crook to get the remains of Rev. Smith, was also killed. The people were kept in constant fear and alarms were of almost daily occurrence.

Wolf/Hillmann

- Migrated: 1877, Dakota Territory.[202]

- Occupation: farmer, 1880, Crook City, Lawrence, Dakota Territory.[12]

- Land Patent: 6 Oct 1881, Crook City, Lawrence, Dakota Territory.[203] Land patent listed as "6N 4E TOWNSHIP SDMTAA 002732" at 44.438° N 103.6191° W Latitude and Longitude

- Resided: working for Douglas Bills from Nankin, Wayne, Michigan, 1894, Yukon, Canadian, Oklahoma Territory.[148]

- Occupation: farmer residing with his wife Hester and son Charles, 1900, Lower False Bottom, Lawrence, South Dakota.[14]

- Resided: 1905, South Dakota.[204]

- Occupation: farmer residing with his wife Ester and daughter Elizabeth, 1910, Lawrence, South Dakota.[16]

- Occupation: farmer residing with his wife Ester and daughter Elizabeth, 1920, Spearfish, Lawrence, South Dakota.[24]

- Moved: with his wife and daughter Elizabeth, about 1924, Detroit, Wayne, Michigan.[205]

- Travel: from The Daily Deadwood Pioneer-Times:, 6 Sep 1926, Deadwood, Lawrence, South Dakota.[205]

   Edmund Wolff of Detroit was an arrival in Deadwood yesterday, coming for the express purpose of assertaining and locating the exact spot at which Rev. Henry Weston Smith (Preacher Smith) met his death in August 1876. Mr. Wolff, who until a couple of years ago had been a resident of the Spearfish valley, where he bad been engaged in farming, left with his wife for Detroit, his old home at that time. Previous to his residence in Spearfish he had lived in Whitewood for a number of years.

- Residence: residing at 8570 Beechdale Ave with his wife Ester and daughter Elizabeth, 1930, Detroit, Wayne, Michigan.[44] This 1,344 square foot house sits on a 5,663 square foot lot and features 1 bathroom. This property was built in 1920.

Wilhelm married **Louise Sophie Koch,** daughter of **Felix Koch**[81] and **Louise Arnold,**[81] on 7 Mar 1882 in Detroit, Wayne, Michigan.[152] Louise was born on 27 Jan 1864 in Inkster, Wayne, Michigan.[14] Another name for Louise was Louise Sophie Wolff.

   Noted events in her life were:
   - Resided: 1880, Romulus, Wayne, Michigan.[12]

The child from this marriage was:
   i. **Charles F. Wolff** was born on 22 May 1884 in Dakota Territory[206] and died on 4 Dec 1950 in Temple City, Los Angeles, California.[207]

Wolf/Hillmann

Noted events in his life were:

- Resided: with father and step-mother, 1900, Lower False Bottom, Lawrence, South Dakota.[14]

- Obituary: from Idaho State Journal, 5 Dec 1950.[208]

Charles Wolff, 66, veteran Union Pacific locomotive engineer, died Monday night in Temple City, Cal. He was taken ill early in September, and he and Mrs. Wolff went to Temple City where a daughter, Mrs. Claude (Beth) Link, is living. Mr. Wolff entered the employ of the Union Pacific Jan. 6, 1910, as a fireman. He was promoted to engineer some six years later. He was a member of lodge 113, Brotherhood of Locomotive Engineers and Firemen. The Wolffs lived for many years at 655 North Fifth and more recently at 244 North Arthur. Mr. Wolff is survived by his widow, Pearl, two daughters, Mrs. Claude Link, Temple City, and Mrs. Ralph (Ruth) Lish, who resides near Los Angeles, and two sisters, one residing in Buffalo, N. Y., and the other in Detroit, Mich. Mr. Wolff was a native of Buffalo. Funeral services will be conducted Thursday in the Hill mortuary in Temple City.

Wilhelm next married **Esther "Et" Maria Bills,** daughter of **William Bills** [153] and **Julia Ann Bogue,** on 9 Jun 1894 in El Reno, Canadian, Oklahoma.[153] Esther was born on 25 Nov 1858 in Nankin, Wayne, Michigan,[209] died on 8 Nov 1933 in Detroit, Wayne, Michigan,[210] and was buried in Grand Lawn Cemetery, Detroit, Wayne, Michigan. Another name for Esther was Ester.

Marriage Notes: The town was in the Choctaw Nation.

Burial Notes: Section 14, Lot 318, Grave 1.

General Notes: Elizabeth became a history teacher in Detroit Public School System, and later chairman, of the history department.

Noted events in her life were:

- Resided: 1880, Nankin, Wayne, Michigan.[12]

- Visited: her brother Douglas Bills, about 1894, Yukon, Canadian, Oklahoma Territory.

- Moved: after 1920, Detroit, Wayne, Michigan. Moved with her husband and one daughter Elizabeth.

The child from this marriage was:

      i. **Elizabeth M. Wolff**[16] was born on 4 Jul 1900 in St. Onge, Lawrence, South Dakota[211] and died on 20 Feb 1996 in Key Biscayne, Dade, Florida.[212]

        Noted events in his life were:
        - Resided: 11319 Manor Pl., 1934, Detroit, Wayne, Michigan.[213]

Wolf/Hillmann

10. Johann Carl Friedrich Wilhelm "William Wallace" Wolf *(Johann Carl Friedrich Theodor "Carl"[1])* was born on 19 Jul 1855 in Fouquettin, Wildberg, Pommern, Preußen,[156] was christened on 30 Jul 1855 in Wildberg, Wildberg, Pommern, Preußen,[157] died on 9 Mar 1934 in Miles City, Custer, Montana,[158] and was buried in Custer County Cemetery, Miles City, Custer, Montana.[56] Another name for Johann was William Wallace Wolff.

Christening Notes: Sponsors: 1. Colonist Johann Genz, 2. farmer wife Emilie Dreyer, 3. girl Wilhelmine Kruse, 4. girl Friederike Schramm

General Notes: He was a freight wagon train driver who worked the route from Bismark to Crook City and Deadwood, Dakota Territory. He was a farmer near Fort Lincoln in Dakota Territory, and a rancher in Montana -- one of the largest in the state -- with 300 sheep on a range along Beaver Creek and the Tongue River.

Noted events in his life were:

• Emigration: on the Donau, 1 May 1858, Hamburg.[23]

• Resided: 1860, Nankin, Wayne, Michigan.[129]

• Residence: 1870, New Buffalo, Berrien, Michigan.[10]

• Occupation: freighter (wagon train driver), 1876.[214]

• Occupation: farmer, 1880, Lincoln, Burleigh, Dakota Territory.[12]

• Event: 1881, Lincoln, Burleigh, Dakota Territory.[214] A flood wipes out his business in Dakota. He moves to Montana.

• Water Rights: On Beaver Creek, a tributary of the Tongue, 30 Dec 1891, Rosebud, Montana.[215]

• Water Rights: On Beaver Creek, a tributary of the Tongue, 2 Mar 1893, Rosebud, Montana.[215]

• Land Patent: Acquires land on the Tongue River south of Brandenberg, 18 Oct 1898, Brandenberg, Custer, Montana.[203]

• Residence: 1900, Township 1, North Range 44 East, Custer, Montana.[14] In the 1900 census William W. Wolff lives in twp 1, range 44. His occupation is stock raising. He and his wife Lucy have been married eight years and have no children. She was born in Michigan in October 1867. Her father was born in Ireland and her mother in New York. His servant is James Standish and his farm hand is George Standish.

• Biography: from an Illustrated History of the Yellowstone Valley, 1907.[214]

    William W. Wolff, who now dwells about eight miles south from Brandenburg, in the Tongue river valley, being in the eastern portion of Rosebud county, was born in Detroit, Michigan, [correction: Prussia] August 19, 1856. His father, Charles Wolff, was born in Germany and came to Michigan when a young man. He had been thoroughly educated and was holding a government position as superintendent of schools [correction: he was a weaver] when he decided to come to the United States. Resigning this, he journeyed to Michigan and there took up farming. In 1886 he removed to Michigan City, Indiana, where he resided until his death in 1906. His wife, Mary (Heldrick) (correction: Hillmann)Wolff, a native of Germany, had died two years before his demise. He was a man of powerful intellect, well trained by liberal education, and was a leader.

Our subject was educated first in the schools of Detroit, and later went to Michigan City where he was engaged in farming. In 1876 Mr. Wolff determined to try the west and so made his way to Bismarck, Dakota, whence he went to Black Hills, which was a mecca of travel at that time, owing to the discovery of gold there a short time previous. He saw an opening in the freighting business and soon had a good outfit and was transferring all kinds of freight from Bismarck to Deadwood and Crook City. It was a very arduous and hazardous business, owing to the many things to contend against. In the first place the Dakota blizzards were enough to frighten an ordinary person from the undertaking, and then, too, the savage Sioux Indians were constantly harassing the whites and killing whenever it was in their power. Despite all this, however, Mr. Wolff pushed ahead and did a fine business. For four years he continued in this business and finally decided that he had sufficient capital to embark in the stock business, which had been his primary object in coming west. He invested and started in business near Bismarck and all went well till one season a gorge was formed in the Missouri by the outgoing ice and so quickly did this dam raise the water that in a few minutes the water was sweeping over the corrals and the house where Mr. Wolff lived. He had two hired hands and they barely escaped by catching an extra boat that was at hand and getting behind some large cottonwood trees to shield themselves from the crushing ice. The water raised to twenty-two feet above the ground where his house was situated and every hoof of stock was swept away. Not a vestige of anything remained but the clothes they had on their backs. All the hard earnings of the years gone by were thus rudely taken from Mr. Wolff, and he was left penniless. He was not a man, however, to sit and cry over the past, but being energetic and resourceful, he soon cast about to find something to put his hand to. He gathered up a herd of mules and brought them to Montana and sold to good advantage and soon had a little working capital on hand again and located the ranch where he now resides -- this was in 1881. He took up sheep raising and later added cattle and is today one of the leading stockmen in this portion of the state. He has had the best of success, and owns one of the finest properties on the Tongue river, it being as well one of the choicest ranches in eastern Montana. Mr. Wolff is a man with the knack of turning his hand to any craft that is necessary to forward the business in hand, and so needing lumber, he bought a small sawmill and cut out all the timber and lumber he needed to construct all his fine buildings and improvements on the ranch and he has the satisfaction of seeing his own handiwork in all that is about him. His place is well improved and is a stimulus to all to build up the country. While all the buildings are good, we would especially mention the barn Mr. Wolff has constructed, which, without doubt, is as fine, if not the finest to be found in this portion of the state. Mr. Wolff has one child, Grace, who was born on the ranch and is now attending school in Miles City.

Mr. Wolff's people are all wealthy. His brother Charles, who was with him in the Black Hills, established one of the first supply depots in that country and had a large freighting outfit. He made money rapidly and after becoming very wealthy, he returned to Michigan City, Indiana, and there resides now.

A man who has had so much experience in the trackless west as Mr. Wolff has had most necessarily much danger to pass through and many hardships to endure. He has faced the savages and had many a fight with them. On one occasion we desire to mention, he was overseeing a large band of beef steers his brother had near Crook City, and it was his custom to ride out, about eight miles, to the camp of the herders to see how things were progressing, once a week. On one occasion, he was accompanied by two friends and the herders warned them to be careful in their return as Indians were skulking around and were hostile. Accordingly they remained in the camp until sundown when they started on their journey back. Their path led them down the famous Whitewood gulch and as they were progressing along this portion they were suddenly fired upon by the savages. The first volley killed one of their number, all of their horses, wounded our subject in the knee and his surviving companion through the hips. Fortunately they escaped being pinned down by the falling horses and were enabled to crawl to a clump of trees. Although the Indians continued to fire upon them they did not receive another bullet while they were making for cover. Mr. Wolff had a rifle and his companion a six-shooter. The rifle, however, became filled with snow in the fall and could not be used at once. The Indians kept up a bombardment and as often as one showed himself in the least, the six shooter did duty to bring him down. Finally our subject got his rifle into trim and the work began in earnest. Several of the Indians were killed and finally after a couple of hour's continuous firing, they gave up the battle and carried off their dead. There were about fifteen Indians, and it is a miracle that the two wounded men were not massacred. Only their skill and pluck saved them. Both were excellent marksmen and this saved them. Many other times Mr. Wolff has been in close quarters but he has always escaped and his fighting qualities have stood him well in hand.

- Water Rights: on Wolf Creek, 10 Oct 1908, Rosebud, Montana.[215]
- Resided: 1910, Township 1, Rosebud, Montana.[16] A rancher and farmer. He is living with his daughter and has a hired hand, Delana Secrest, a sheep herder.
- Resided: 1920, District 26, Rosebud, Montana.[24] A rancher with no family members lived with him. He had a housekeeper, a boarder, and four hired men.
- Event: Announcement of the Annual Woolgrowers Convention, 12 Jan 1928, Billings, Christian, Missouri.[216] Attendance of more than 500 expected. William Wolff's name is mentioned in the article.
- Land Patent: 25 Apr 1928, Brandenberg, Rosebud, Montana.[203] Aqcuired property is on the west side of the Tongue River bear Brandenberg.
- Resided: 1930, Brandenberg, Rosebud, Montana.[44] A sheep rancher living with his new wife and step daughter. He has two hired hands.
- Land Patent: 8 Dec 1932, Brandenberg, Rosebud, Montana.[203] Acquired property is on the northwest side of the Tongue River near Brandenberg.

Johann married **Lucille Perry,** daughter of **James S. Perry** and **Mary Jane Fries,** on 17 Feb 1892 in Mount Clemens, Macomb, Michigan.[159] Lucille was born on 27 Oct 1864 in Mount Clemens, Harrison, Macomb, Michigan[217] and died on 30 May 1951 in Billings, Yellowstone, Montana.[218] Another name for Lucille was Lucy Wolff.

Noted events in her life were:
- Resided: 1900, Custer, Montana.[14]

The child from this marriage was:
   i. **Grace Estella Wolff** was born on 20 Aug 1894 in Brandenberg, Custer, Montana[219]

Wolf/Hillmann

and died on 18 Oct 1997 in Sandres, Calaveras, California.

Grace married **James Henry Slaton** on 30 Aug 1911 in Miles City, Custer, Montana.[219] James was born in 1883 in Bismarck, Burleigh, North Dakota.[219]

Grace next married **William F. Suepke** on 18 Dec 1928 in Miles City, Custer, Montana.[219] William was born in 1888 in Minnesota.[219]

Johann next married **Rose Elizabeth Shannon**,[160] daughter of **John Shannon**[220] and **Mary Coffey**,[220] on 7 Dec 1929 in Big Timber, Sweet Grass, Montana.[161] Rose was born on 19 Oct 1886 in Preble, Fillmore, Minnesota[221] and died on 24 Nov 1966 in Miles City, Custer, Montana.[222]

Minahan/O'Brien in America

First Generation

11. John Minahan[32] was born circa 1834 in Ireland.[223] Another name for John was John Moynahan.

Noted events in his life were:
- Religion: Roman Catholic.

- Resided: 1854, Croom, Limerick, Ireland.[224]

- Immigrated: to America, about 1866.[9] There is a John Minehan on the *SS City of New York* arriving in New York on 16 April 1866, however it is not proven that this is the same John Minahan.

- Occupation: stonecutter, 1870, Eastchester, Westchester, New York.[10]

- Resided: about 1872, New York.[12]

- Occupation: stonecutter residing at 26 Grand, 1875, Hartford, Hartford, Connecticut.[37]

- Occupation: stonecutter residing at 27 Grand, 1876, Hartford, Hartford, Connecticut.[37]

- Citizenship: application filed, 13 Oct 1876, Yonkers, Westchester, New York.[225] Witnessed by Denis Murphy and John Murphy. Form originally filled out as Millihan, then crossed out and corrected to Moynihan. Signed with an X.

- Inmate: almshouse for two nights, 18 Nov 1876, Albany, Albany, New York.[226] "for want of labor."

- Occupation: stonecutter residing at 41 Chestnut, 1879, Albany, Albany, New York.[37]

- Occupation: stonecutter residing at 336 State St., 1880, Albany, Albany, New York.[227]

- Occupation: stonecutter residing at 47 High, 1883, Albany, Albany, New York.[37]

- Occupation: stonecutter residing at 85 Elk, 1885, Albany, Albany, New York.[37]

- Occupation: stonecutter residing at 2624 K NW, 1889, Washington, District of Columbia.[37] Lived with his son Michael.

- Occupation: stonecutter, 1891-1901, Cincinnati, Hamilton, Ohio.[24]

John married **Mary O'Brien**[32] on 8 Oct 1854 in St. Mary of the Assumption Church, Croom, Limerick, Ireland.[228] Mary was born circa 1834 in Limerick, Ireland,[229] died on 18 Jun 1879 in Albany, Albany, New York,[230] and was buried in St. Mary's, Albany, Albany, New York.[231] The cause of her death was carcinoma of uterus.

> Marriage Notes: The witnesses to the marriage were Matthew Moloney and Mary Minahan. Fr. James O'Shea celebrated the wedding as curate of Croom parish.
>
> Death Notes: 44 Chestnut Street in Albany, New York.
>
> Burial Notes: She was probably removed to another cemetery when St. Mary's was closed. The land is now a high school.
>
> Noted events in her life were:
> - Religion: Roman Catholic.

Minahan/O'Brien

- Immigrated: to America, est 1866.
- Travel: 16 Jul 1868, New York.[9] on *SS Virginia* from Ireland
- Travel: 7 Sep 1869, New York, New York.[9] Returns to New York on the ship *SS Virginia* after a visit to Ireland.
- Resided: 1870, Eastchester, Westchester, New York.[10]

Children from this marriage were:

12   i. **Michael E. Minahan** was born in Aug 1855 in Croom, Limerick, Ireland,[184] was christened on 26 Aug 1855 in St. Mary of the Assumption Church, Croom, Limerick, Ireland,[232] died on 3 Oct 1924 in Tarrytown, Westchester, New York,[233] and was buried in Sleepy Hollow Cemetery, Tarrytown, Westchester, New York.[234]

Michael married **Margaret McIntyre** (b. Aug 1863, d. 5 Aug 1946) about 1888.[14]

ii. **Patrick Minahan** was christened on 23 May 1857 in St. Mary of the Assumption Church, Croom, Limerick, Ireland[235] and died on 17 Oct 1935 in Manhattan, New York, New York.[236] Another name for Patrick was Patrick Moynahan. He had no relationships and no children.

Christening Notes: Godparents were Patrick O'Brien and Mary Cronin. The priest was Rev. Michael Gleeson, curate of Croom parish from 1856 to 1857.

Noted events in his life were:
- Travel: on the ship Virgina from Ireland, 7 Sep 1869, New York, New York.[237]
- Resided: 1870, Eastchester, Westchester, New York.[10]
- Occupation: sculptor residing at 2604 1/2 L NW, 1889, Washington, District of Columbia.[37]
- Occupation: carver living at 221 East 30th, 1891, New York, New York, New York.[37]
- Occupation: sculptor residing at 83 Superior, 1925, Toledo, Lucas, Ohio.[37]
- Occupation: sculptor, 1930, Manhattan, New York, New York.[44]

iii. **Joseph Minahan** was christened on 1 Feb 1859 in St. Mary of the Assumption Church, Croom, Limerick, Ireland.[238]

Research Notes: Probably died as infant.

iv. **Joseph Minahan** was christened on 8 Feb 1863 in St. Mary of the Assumption Church, Croom, Limerick, Ireland[239] and died on 19 Apr 1898 in Boston, Suffolk, Massachusetts.[240] Another name for Joseph was Joseph Moynahan.

Christening Notes: Godparents were Soloman O'Brien and Catherine O'Brien. The priest was John Quinlan, parish priest of Croom from 1862 to 1892.

Death Notes: Died of aortic and mitral regurgitation at the City Hospital on Laconia St.

Noted events in his life were:
- Arrived: on Virgina, 16 Jul 1868, New York.[9]
- Resided: 1870, Eastchester, Westchester, New York.[10]
- Resided: 1880, Albany, Albany, New York.[12]

Minahan/O'Brien

- Occupation: architectural sculptor, Moynahan Brothers at 520 Albany, 1883, Boston, Suffolk, Massachusetts.[37]

v. **John Moynahan** was born about 1866.[241]

Research Notes: He may have been born in New York. John did not appear in the 1880 census with his father, so either he died or was taken in by another family when his mother died.

Noted events in his life were:
- Travel: 7 Sep 1869, New York, New York.[9] on the ship *SS Virginia* from Ireland

- Resided: 1870, Eastchester, Westchester, New York.[10]

vi. **Thomas Francis Moynahan** was born on 29 Aug 1868 in Mt. Vernon, Westchester, New York[10] and was christened on 6 Sep 1868 in Immaculate Conception Church, Tuckahoe, Westchester, New York.[242]

Christening Notes: The sponsors were Patrick Shanley and Sarah Hawks; the priest was Reverend John McEvoy. Parents are listed as John Moynahan and Mary O'Brien. First child baptized in the church.

Research Notes: Thomas did not appear in the 1880 census with his father, so either he died or was taken in by another family.

Noted events in his life were:
- Travel: on the ship Virgina from Ireland, 7 Sep 1869, New York, New York.[9]

- Resided: 1870, Eastchester, Westchester, New York.[10]

vii. **May Moynahan** was born in 1872 in New York.[12]

Research Notes: In 1900, she is possibly a domestic servant in the home of Thomas J. Dunn at 152 127th St., Manhattan. There is a May Moynihan, a domestic servant in Manhattan, who died on 30 Dec 1921, but her death certificate gives her father as Dennis, not John.

Noted events in her life were:
- Resided: 1880, Albany, Albany, New York.[12]

- Occupation: servant in the home of Thomas J. Dunn at 152 127th St, 1900, Manhattan, New York, New York.[14]

viii. **William S. Moynahan**[243] was born on 15 Aug 1873 in New York,[244] died on 4 Oct 1938 in Cleveland, Cuyahoga, Ohio,[243] and was buried on 7 Oct 1938 in Alger Cemetery, Cleveland, Cuyahoga, Ohio.[245] The cause of his death was Pulmonary tuberculosis.

Birth Notes: William self-reports that he was born in New York City, New York, but more likely he was born in nearby Westchester County.

Death Notes: Parents listed as John Moynahan and Mary O'Brien.

Medical Notes: His death may have been related to stone dust. From a medical report: "The data conclusively indicate an excessive proportionate mortality from pulmonary tuberculosis among marble and stone cutters at every divisional period of life."[246]

Noted events in his life were:
- Resided: 1880, Albany, Albany, New York.[12]

- Occupation: stonecutter residing at 481 H SW, 1897, Washington, District of Columbia.[37]

- Occupation: stone carver residing at 360 Broad St., 1900, Newark, Essex, New Jersey.[14]

- Resided: 1911, Cincinnati, Hamilton, Ohio.[247]

- Employment: stone carver at J. W. Hoadley Stone Company, 1915, Bloomington, Monroe, Indiana.[248]

- Employment: from Bloomington Evening World, 8 Sep 1915.[249]

　　William S. Moynahan left today for Cleveland, Ohio, where be is going to do some stone carving on the new high school building.

- Occupation: sculptor residing at 7020 Lorain Av, 1916, Cleveland, Cuyahoga, Ohio.[37]

- Occupation: stone carver residing at 3308 W 90th, 1917, Cleveland, Cuyahoga, Ohio.[37]

- Occupation: cutter residing at 410 S Main Ave., 1918, Sioux Falls, Minnehaha, South Dakota.[37]

- Resided: on 9th St., 1920, Lorain, Lorain, Ohio.[24]

- Occupation: stone carver residing at 303 W 102d, 1921, Cleveland, Cuyahoga, Ohio.[37]

- Office: secretary of independent stone cutter's union, 1922, Amherst, Lorain, Ohio.[250]

- Occupation: sculptor at 3393 E Scarborough Rd C H, 1923, Cleveland, Cuyahoga, Ohio.[37]

- Occupation: stone carver residing at 3393 E Scarborough Rd., 1925-1928, Cleveland, Cuyahoga, Ohio.[37]

- Occupation: sculptor at stone company, 1930, Cleveland Heights, Cuyahoga, Ohio.[251]

- Obituary: from Stonecutters Journal, Nov 1938.[252]

　　MOYNAHAN - William S., another member of our Cleveland (Ohio) Local, died October 4th, at the Cleveland City Hospital, aged 64 years. He had been ill for more than six years. Brother Moynahan was born in New York City, coming from a family that for several generations had been engaged in sculpturing and carving and many fine examples of his work are to be seen in and around Cleveland. While still in the east, before locating in Ohio some twenty odd years ago, he did some outstanding work for the Yale and Duke Universities, and for the Library of Congress, at Washington. He is survived by his widow and two daughters, to whom the members of Cleveland Local extend their sympathy.

William married **Harriet Rose Jolly**,[253] daughter of **William Perry Jolly**[129] and **Harriet Catherine Selby**,[254] on 27 Dec 1902 in Marion, Grant, Indiana.[253] Harriet was born on 15 Aug 1859 in Alexandria, Campbell, Kentucky,[255] died on 7 May 1915 in Cincinnati, Hamilton, Ohio,[248] and was buried in Greenlawn Cemetery, Newport, Campbell, Kentucky.[248]

Noted events in her life were:

• Resided: 1860, Alexandria, Campbell, Kentucky.[129]

• Resided: 1870, Covington, Kenton, Kentucky.[10]

• Resided: 1880, Newport, Campbell, Kentucky.[12]

• Obituary: from the Bloomington (Indiana) Weekly Courier, 11 May 1915.[248]

DETAILS OF MRS. MOYNAHAN'S DEATH

William S. Moynahan, whose wife died in Cincinnati last Friday night, was in Bloomington Sunday getting a number of articles which Mrs. Moynahan had carefully prepared and put away here for burial purposes. It was her dying request that she be clothed in her own wearing apparel.

The many Bloomington and Bedford friends of Mrs. Moynahan will be pained to learn that she suffered terribly during the closing days of her life. Everything that could possibly be done, however, was done for her comfort, and she was attended by five physicians of Cincinnati and given the best of hospital attention. She was cheerful and conscious up until the very last, often singing favorite hymns and praying to her Master.

Her case was most puzzling to the physicians and an x-ray examination was made two weeks ago. The photograph did not reveal entirely her trouble, and a post mortem was held Saturday. This disclosed that her death was caused by cirrhosis of the liver, and the kidneys were also diseased.

The body was removed today to the home of her sister at 2217 Kenton Street, Walnut Hills, from where the funeral will be held tomorrow morning at ten o'clock. Interment will be in Greenlawn Cemetery at Newport, Ky.

Mr. Moynahan will return to Bloomington the latter part of the week to resume his work with the J. W. Hoadley Stone Company.

William next married **Anna Rainerman**,[256] daughter of **Bernard John Rainerman**[257] and **Harmke Bess**,[257] on 20 Dec 1915 in Franklin, Ohio.[257] Anna was born on 31 Mar 1880 in Amsterdam, Holland[257] and died on 23 Jun 1949 in Lakewood, Cuyahoga, Ohio.[258]

Noted events in her life were:

• Immigrated: 1886.[24]

• Obituary: from the Cleveland Press, 25 Jun 1949.[56]

Moynahan, Anna, beloved wife of the late William S.; mother of Irene Oviatt and the late Laverna Haeflinger; residence, 4927 East Park Dr., North Olmsted; beloved sister of William Ramerman, Harry Ramerman (deceased), Herman Feitman (deceased), Mrs. George Leber, Mrs. Arthur Bourne, Miss Jen Ramerman, Barney Ramerman, Mrs. Leopard Radcliffe and Mrs. Harvey Koelliker. Friends may call at the Branch-Kauffman Funeral Home, 16605 Detroit Ave., Lakewood, where services will be held Saturday, June 25, at 2 p. m.

----

ix. **Edward T. Moynahan** was born on 27 Apr 1875 in Hartford, Hartford, Connecticut[259] and died on 12 Jun 1911 in Tewksbury, Middlesex, Massachusetts.[240] The cause of his death was chronic kidney disease.

Minahan/O'Brien

Death Notes: Parents listed as John Moynahan and Mary O'Brien.

Noted events in his life were:
- Resided: 1880, Albany, Albany, New York.[12]

- Occupation: stone carver, 1903, Boston, Suffolk, Massachusetts.[37] Living at 93 Villiage and working at 27 Knapp.

- Occupation: peddler, 1911, Massachusetts.[240]

13   x.   **Mary E. Moynahan** was born on 24 Aug 1876 in New York,[104] died on 9 Feb 1920 in Detroit, Wayne, Michigan,[105] and was buried on 12 Feb 1920 in Woodlawn Cemetery, Detroit, Wayne, Michigan.[105]

Mary married **Oscar Christian Weidemann** (b. 1 Aug 1871, d. 9 Feb 1920) on 19 May 1901 in Buffalo, Erie, New York.[32]

(Duplicate Line. See Person 3)

Minahan/O'Brien

Second Generation (Children)

12. Michael E. Minahan *(John [1])* was born in Aug 1855 in Croom, Limerick, Ireland,[184] was christened on 26 Aug 1855 in St. Mary of the Assumption Church, Croom, Limerick, Ireland,[232] died on 3 Oct 1924 in Tarrytown, Westchester, New York,[233] and was buried in Sleepy Hollow Cemetery, Tarrytown, Westchester, New York.[234] Another name for Michael was Michael E. Moynahan.

Christening Notes: Godparents were John Grady and Honora O'Brien.

Burial Notes: Lot 3019, section 54.

Noted events in his life were:
- Immigrated: to America, est 1866.[14]

- Resided: 1870, Eastchester, Westchester, New York.[10]

- Occupation: stone cutter residing at 26 Grand, 1875, Hartford, Hartford, Connecticut.[37]

- Occupation: stone cutter residing at 29 Green, 1876, Hartford, Hartford, Connecticut.[37]

- Occupation: stone cutter residing at 41 Chestnut, 1879, Albany, Albany, New York.[37]

- Occupation: stone cutter residing at 336 State, 1880, Albany, Albany, New York.[37]

- Occupation: architectural sculptor, Moynahan Brothers at 520 Albany living at 6 Ferdinand, 1883, Boston, Suffolk, Massachusetts.[37]

- Occupation: sculptor residing at 2624 K NW, 1889, Washington, District of Columbia.[37] Lived with his father and near his brother Patrick.

- Occupation: church sextan, 1900, Mt. Pleasant, North Tarrytown, Westchester, New York.[14]

- Occupation: janitor, 1905, Mt. Pleasant, North Tarrytown, Westchester, New York.[260]

- Occupation: janitor at school, 1915, Mt. Pleasant, North Tarrytown, Westchester, New York.[261]

- Occupation: janitor church us census, 1920, North Tarrytown, Westchester, New York.[24] St. Teresa's Church

- Obituary: from the Yonkers Statesman, 4 Oct 1924.[262]

Old Tarrytown Resident Dies While at Work
   Tarrytown -- While crowds of workers in the Chevtolet automobile factory here looked on, the Rev. Father Hogan, of St. Teresa's Church, adminsitered the last rites to Michael Monahan, for more than 20 years sexton of the church and one of the most popular of Tarrytown residents, who died shortly after being suddenly stricken with a paralytic stroke yesterday.
   The noon-hour of crowds of shop workers were hurrying home when Monahan collapsed on the shipping platform. His pastor was called and he died in the arms of a fellow worker. He was 60 years old.

Minahan/O'Brien

Michael married **Margaret McIntyre** about 1888.[14] Margaret was born in Aug 1863 in Ireland,[14] died on 5 Aug 1946, and was buried in Sleepy Hollow Cemetery, Tarrytown, Westchester, New York.

> Noted events in her life were:
> * Immigrated: 1877.[14]
>
> * Resided: 1940, Mt. Pleasant, North Tarrytown, Westchester, New York.[71]

Children from this marriage were:

> i. **Thomas F. Monahan** was born in Jun 1890 in New York.
>
> ii. **William V. Monahan** was born on 10 Jul 1893 in Mt. Pleasant, North Tarrytown, Westchester, New York,[180] died on 25 Oct 1957, and was buried in Sleepy Hollow Cemetery, Tarrytown, Westchester, New York.
>
>> Noted events in his life were:
>> * Occupation: mason, 1918, North Tarrytown, Westchester, New York.[37]
>>
>> * Resided: 1940, Mt. Pleasant, North Tarrytown, Westchester, New York.[71]
>
> iii. **Susan Elizabeth Monahan**[263] was born on 30 Aug 1895 in New York[24] and died in Mar 1985 in Hollywood, Broward, Florida.
>
>> Noted events in her life were:
>> * Resided: 1940, Mt. Pleasant, North Tarrytown, Westchester, New York.[71]
>
> Susan married **Archibald Barr,** son of **John Barr** and **Elizabeth McKee,** on 30 Mar 1913 in North Tarrytown, Westchester, New York.[264] Archibald was born on 18 Dec 1890 in New York[24] and died in 1958 in Franklin, Massachusetts.
>
> Susan next married **John Skitmas**[56] after 1958.

13. Mary E. Moynahan *(John [1])* was born on 24 Aug 1876 in New York,[104] died on 9 Feb 1920 in Detroit, Wayne, Michigan,[105] and was buried on 12 Feb 1920 in Woodlawn Cemetery, Detroit, Wayne, Michigan.[105]

> Christening Notes: Ann Sullivan was godmother at baptism.
>
> General Notes:
>   Mary claims in her marriage license that she was born in New York City, New York, but more likely she was born in nearby Westchester County, New York. She was disabled, perhaps having a club foot.
>   She is listed as Mary E. Lardner in the 1880 Albany census, in the same home as her widowed father John Moynahan and her siblings. According to the Albany city archives, Mrs. Lardner had only one daughter, Anne, so Mary. E. Larner was Mary E. Moynahan. After her father left Albany, she stayed with the McNamara family.
>   It is not known how Oscar and Mary first met, but they were married in Buffalo, New York in 1901. After their daughter, Alma, was born in Erie in 1904, they moved to Detroit in 1905 where Oscar worked as a painter with his father.
>   In 1920, Mary was murdered by her husband.[49]

> Noted events in her life were:
> * Religion: Roman Catholic.
>
> * Resided: 1880, Albany, Albany, New York.[12]
>
> * Resided: with William and Emma McNamara, 1892, Albany, Albany, New

York.[106] Mary does not appear with them in the 1900 census.

- Resided: after May 1901, Erie, Erie, Pennsylvania.[32]

- Resided: at 1394 Belvidere, 1910, Detroit, Wayne, Michigan.[16]

- Resided: at 1394 Belvidere, 1920, Detroit, Wayne, Michigan.[24]

- Cause of death: by murder, shot by her husband., 9 Feb 1920, Detroit, Wayne, Michigan.[107]

Mary married **Oscar Christian Weidemann,** son of **Christian Heinrich Johannes Weidemann**[1] and **Maria Sophia Caroline Christine Wolf,** on 19 May 1901 in Buffalo, Erie, New York.[32] Oscar was born on 1 Aug 1871 in Detroit, Wayne, Michigan,[31] died on 9 Feb 1920 in Detroit, Wayne, Michigan,[26] and was buried on 12 Feb 1920 in Woodlawn Cemetery, Detroit, Wayne, Michigan.[4]

General Notes: Oscar grew up in Detroit. He studied art in New York and won a scholarship for a year at the Royal Academy of Art in Berlin. He started a decorating business in Erie, Pennsylvania about 1901. He and his wife moved to Detroit about 1905 where he worked with his father as a painter.

Noted events in his life were:
- Resided: at 44 Croghan (Monroe), 1880, Detroit, Wayne, Michigan.[12]

- Education: completed 8th grade at Washington School (Detroit Public Schools), 24 Jun 1887, Detroit, Wayne, Michigan.[92] Admitted to Detroit High School.

- Education: studying art, about 1891-1893, New York.[93]

- Occupation: painter living with his father, 1891, Detroit, Wayne, Michigan.[94]

- Event: applied for a passport, 10 Oct 1893, New York, New York, New York.[95]

- Arrival: about Nov 1893, Hamburg.[96]

- Arrival: from Hamberg, 6 Nov 1893, Berlin, Germany.[96]

- Education: attended Königliche Kunstschule zu Berlin (Royal Art School in Berlin), about 11 Nov 1893-Nov 1894, Berlin, Germany.[97] Now part of the University of the Arts Berlin.

- Travel: travels to several cities, Jun 1894-Aug 1894, Germany.[96]

- Travel: visits his father's hometown, 6 Aug 1894 to 8 Aug 1894, Neustadt, Schleswig-Holstein, Germany.[96] His sketch of a home at Waschgraben 27 may indicate that his father or a relative lived there.

- Newspaper Article: Detroit Free Press, 30 Sep 1894.[97]

    Among the seventy-nine pupils who attended the Royal School of Art at Berlin during the last semester, nineteen passed the examination. Oscar C. Weidemann of Detroit was one of these, and was also awarded a premium. After studying several years in New York, Mr. Weidemann went to Europe, where he intends to complete his art studies.

- Departure: 17 Feb 1895, Hamburg.[98] on the *SS Russia*

- Arrival: 4 Mar 1895, New York, New York, New York.[9] from Hamburg on the

SS Russia after a year abroad studying art.

- Residence: 141 W 13th street next door to Anna Sullivan (godmother of his child), before 1900-1901, Erie, Erie, Pennsylvania.[99]

- Residence: 1016 W. 6th (home), 710 State (office in 1903), 1902-1904, Erie, Erie, Pennsylvania.[100]

- Occupation: decorator residing at 1394 Belvidere, 1910, Detroit, Wayne, Michigan.[16]

- Occupation: painter residing at 1394 Belvidere, 1915, Detroit, Wayne, Michigan.[37]

- Occupation: painter in a paint shop residing at at 1394 Belvidere, 1920, Detroit, Wayne, Michigan.[24]

- Cause of death: from The Detroit News, 9 Feb 1920, Detroit, Wayne, Michigan.[101]

  Girl Hears Shots Finds Dying Parents
  Oscar Weidemann, 1294 Belvidere avenue, shot his wife Mary and then turned his revolver on himself, Sunday night, inflicting the wounds of which both died early today at Receiving Hospital. Their daughter, 17 years old, heard the shots and running from a bedroom saw their bodies lying on the floor. She rushed screaming to neighbors, who notified police.

  Weidemann is believed to have been demented. He left a letter accusing his wife, his mother, his relatives and neighbors generally, and describing quarrels. The letter said he had been in Receiving Hospital for alcoholism.

  According to Mrs. Eleanor Neville, next door, they heard the two shots and turned out the lights, fearing he might fire through their windows. Neighbors describe Mrs. Weidemann as a charming woman of 38, crippled, so she could seldom leave the house. They said that Weidemann was jealous, never allowing his wife or daughter to associate with neighbors or, even if he could help it, to walk up Gratiot avenue.

  Weidemann's letter indicated he had furious quarrels with neighbors over rabbits and chickens invading his yard.

  The daughter is being cared for by her grandmother, Mrs. Mary Weidemann, who is in serious condition as a result of a fall sustained a week ago.

- Cause of death: from The Detroit Free Press, 10 Feb 1920, Detroit, Wayne, Michigan.[102]

  Woman Murdered by Husband who Turns Gun on Himself
  Oscar Weideman, dying, Found with Pistol in Hand
  A double shooting, in which Mrs. Mary Weideman, of 1394 Bevidere avenue, was killed by her husband, Oscar, who then turned the weapon on himslf, inflicting what is believed to be a mortal wound.

  According to the story told to the police by Alma Weideman, daughter of the principals in the shooting affair, she had gone to bed and her mother was following her, when she heard something on the stairway outside her room. She hurried out and found her mother on the floor at the foot of the steps. He father lay a short distance away, clasping a pistol in his hand. Both were shot though the head. When the police arrived they found another pistol in Weideman's top pocket.

     Believed to be Demented

     The pair were taken to the Receiving hospital where Mrs. Weideman died at an early hour this morning. Mr. Weideman was not expected to live.

     Police believe that Weideman was demented. He is said to have undergone treatment some years ago for mental trouble.

- Memoriam: Sep 1922.[103] $50 donation made in his honor to *The Painter and Decorator* journal.

(Duplicate Line. See Person 3)

Ancestor Chart and Report Explained

The ancestor chart and report start with Alma Marie Weidemann and follow all lines of her ancestry back to Germany and Ireland.

The charts are connected by chart numbers. Look for chart numbers in the upper right hand corner. The "continued on chart" numbers run down the right hand side.

The ancestor report uses "ahnentafel" numbers. Ahnentafel means "ancestor table" in German. In an ahnentafel report, a father's number is double the child's number and the mother's number is the father's number plus 1. Alma Marie Weidemann is assigned the number 1. Her father and mother are assigned the numbers 2 and 3 and her father's parents are assigned 4 and 5. If you open a random page and find someone with the number 20, then the parents' numbers are 40 and 41 and the child's number is 10. Once the reader is accustomed to ahnentafel numbers, it becomes very easy move up and down from parent to child and vice versa.

This shows how the numbering system works:

```
                        8. great-grandfather
          4. paternal grandfather
                        9. great-grandmother
     2. father
                        10. great-grandfather
          5. paternal grandmother
                        11. great-grandmother
1. root
                        12. great-grandfather
          6. maternal grandfather
                        13. great-grandmother
     3. mother
                        14. great-grandfather
          7. maternal grandmother
                        15. great-grandfather
```

The chart contains only Alma's ancestors, but the report includes her ancestors' children. Newspaper articles and obituaries are also part of the report.

Ancestor Chart

8 Claus Friederich Weidemann[1]   cont. 2
b. 10 Dec 1801 [265]
p. Stolpe, Holstein
m. 21 Mar 1824 [266]
p. Neustadt, Holstein
d. 9 Mar 1881 [1]
p. Neustadt, Holstein

4 Christian Heinrich J Weidemann[1]
b. 26 Feb 1837 [2]
p. Neustadt, Holstein
m. 6 Feb 1868 [19]
p. Detroit, Wayne, Michigan
d. 22 Jun 1913 [3]
p. Detroit, Wayne, Michigan

9 Anna Catherina Hedewig Ahrend[1]   3
b. 1797 [267]
p. Klenau, Holstein
d. 26 Jan 1846 [1]
p. Neustadt, Holstein

2 Oscar Christian Weidemann
b. 1 Aug 1871 [31]
p. Detroit, Wayne, Michigan
m. 19 May 1901 [32]
p. Buffalo, Erie, New York
d. 9 Feb 1920 [26]
p. Detroit, Wayne, Michigan

10 Johann Carl Friedrich Theodor Wolf4
b. 7 Dec 1814 [122]
p. Zwiedorf, Mecklenburg-Schwerin
m. about 1836 [132]
p.
d. 20 Mar 1906 [124]
p. Michigan City, LaPorte, Indiana

5 Maria Sophia Caroline Christine Wolf
b. 3 Aug 1841 [20]
p. Wolkow, Pommern, Preußen
d. 14 Mar 1928 [22]
p. Detroit, Wayne, Michigan

11 Johanna Sophia Elisabeth Hillmann 5
b. 31 May 1811 [133]
p. Galenbeck, Mecklenburg-Schwerin
d. 16 Dec 1903 [135]
p. Michigan City, LaPorte, Indiana

1 Alma Marie Weidemann
b. 19 Apr 1904 [108]
p. Erie, Erie, Pennsylvania
m. 22 Jan 1928
p. Detroit, Wayne, Michigan
d. 26 Aug 2004 [110]
p. Ann Arbor, Washtenaw, Michigan
sp. Ewald Conrad Swanson M. D.

12
b.
p.
m.
p.
d.
p.

13
b.
p.
d.
p.

6 John Minahan [32]
b. circa 1834 [223]
p. Ireland
m. 8 Oct 1854 [228]
p. St. Mary of the Assumption Church, C~
d.
p.

3 Mary E. Moynahan
b. 24 Aug 1876 [104]
p. New York
d. 9 Feb 1920 [105]
p. Detroit, Wayne, Michigan

14
b.
p.
m.
p.
d.
p.

7 Mary O'Brien [32]
b. circa 1834 [229]
p. Limerick, Ireland
d. 18 Jun 1879 [230]
p. Albany, Albany, New York

15
b.
p.
d.
p.

Ancestor Chart

No. 1 on this chart is the same as no. 8 on chart no. 1

8 Hans Hinrich Weidemann[1]   cont. 6
b. about 1714[1]
p. Kassau, Holstein
m. 6 Nov 1746[1]
p. Altenkrempe, Holstein
d. 11 Jan 1798[1]
p. Stolpe, Holstein

9 Maria Elisabeth Schumacher[1]   cont. 7
b. about 1715[1]
p. Sierhagen, Holstein
d. 25 Apr 1792[1]
p. Stolpe, Holstein

4 Hans Hinrich Weidemann[1]
c. 7 Jan 1748[1]
p. Stolpe, Holstein
m. 12 Oct 1776[1]
p. Altenkrempe, Holstein
d. 13 Jan 1812[1]
p. Stolpe, Holstein

10 Hinrich Schumacher[1]
b.
p.
m.
p.
d.
p.

5 Anna Margaretha Schumacher[1]
c. 19 Jul 1746[1]
p. Kassau, Holstein
d. 16 Dec 1818[1]
p. Kassau, Holstein

11 Hedwig Wehde[1]   cont. 8
b.
p.
d.
p.

2 Claus Hinrich Weidemann[1]
b. 8 May 1780[1]
p. Stolpe, Holstein
m. 11 Oct 1800[1]
p. Altenkrempe, Holstein
d. 1 Dec 1857[1]
p. Kassau, Holstein

1 Claus Friederich Weidemann[1]
b. 10 Dec 1801 [265]
p. Stolpe, Holstein
m. 21 Mar 1824 [266]
p. Neustadt, Holstein
d. 9 Mar 1881[1]
p. Neustadt, Holstein
sp. Anna Catherina Hedewig Ahrend[1]

12
b.
p.
m.
p.
d.
p.

6 Hans Detlef Haack[1]
b.
p.
m. circa 1775[1]
p.
d.
p.

13
b.
p.
d.
p.

3 Anna Elsabe Dorothea Haack[1]
b. 30 Jun 1777[1]
p. Kassau, Holstein
d. 2 Feb 1855[1]
p. Kassau, Holstein

14
b.
p.
m.
p.
d.
p.

7 Anna Elsabe Diekmann[1]
b.
p.
d.
p.

15
b.
p.
d.
p.

Ancestor Chart

No. 1 on this chart is the same as no. 9 on chart no. 1

2 Hans Jürgen Ahrend [1]
b. 1766 [268]
p.
m.
p.
d.
p.

1 Anna Catherina Hedewig Ahrend [1]
b. 1797 [267]
p. Klenau, Holstein
m. 21 Mar 1824 [266]
p. Neustadt, Holstein
d. 26 Jan 1846 [1]
p. Neustadt, Holstein
sp. Claus Friederich Weidemann [1]

3 Margaretha Elisabeth Westphal [1]
b. 1765 [267]
p.
d.
p.

4
b.
p.
m.
p.
d.
p.

5
b.
p.
d.
p.

6
b.
p.
m.
p.
d.
p.

7
b.
p.
d.
p.

8
b.
p.
m.
p.
d.
p.

9
b.
p.
d.
p.

10
b.
p.
m.
p.
d.
p.

11
b.
p.
d.
p.

12
b.
p.
m.
p.
d.
p.

13
b.
p.
d.
p.

14
b.
p.
m.
p.
d.
p.

15
b.
p.
d.
p.

Ancestor Chart

No. 1 on this chart is the same as no. 10 on chart no. 1

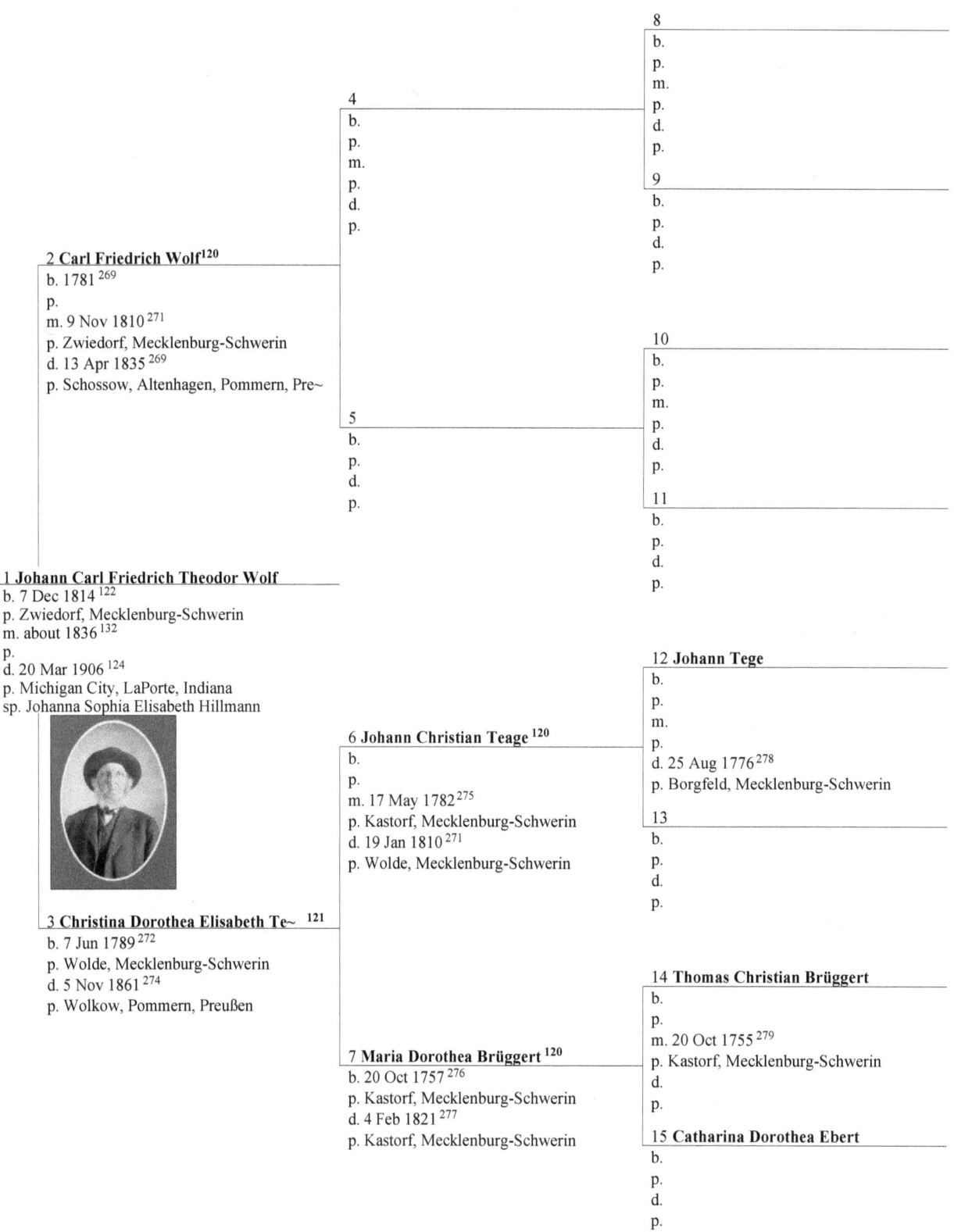

2 Carl Friedrich Wolf[120]
b. 1781 [269]
p.
m. 9 Nov 1810 [271]
p. Zwiedorf, Mecklenburg-Schwerin
d. 13 Apr 1835 [269]
p. Schossow, Altenhagen, Pommern, Pre~

1 Johann Carl Friedrich Theodor Wolf
b. 7 Dec 1814 [122]
p. Zwiedorf, Mecklenburg-Schwerin
m. about 1836 [132]
p.
d. 20 Mar 1906 [124]
p. Michigan City, LaPorte, Indiana
sp. Johanna Sophia Elisabeth Hillmann

3 Christina Dorothea Elisabeth Te~ [121]
b. 7 Jun 1789 [272]
p. Wolde, Mecklenburg-Schwerin
d. 5 Nov 1861 [274]
p. Wolkow, Pommern, Preußen

4
b.
p.
m.
p.
d.
p.

5
b.
p.
d.
p.

6 Johann Christian Teage [120]
b.
p.
m. 17 May 1782 [275]
p. Kastorf, Mecklenburg-Schwerin
d. 19 Jan 1810 [271]
p. Wolde, Mecklenburg-Schwerin

7 Maria Dorothea Brüggert [120]
b. 20 Oct 1757 [276]
p. Kastorf, Mecklenburg-Schwerin
d. 4 Feb 1821 [277]
p. Kastorf, Mecklenburg-Schwerin

8
b.
p.
m.
p.
d.
p.

9
b.
p.
d.
p.

10
b.
p.
m.
p.
d.
p.

11
b.
p.
d.
p.

12 Johann Tege
b.
p.
m.
p.
d. 25 Aug 1776 [278]
p. Borgfeld, Mecklenburg-Schwerin

13
b.
p.
d.
p.

14 Thomas Christian Brüggert
b.
p.
m. 20 Oct 1755 [279]
p. Kastorf, Mecklenburg-Schwerin
d.
p.

15 Catharina Dorothea Ebert
b.
p.
d.
p.

Ancestor Chart

No. 1 on this chart is the same as no. 11 on chart no. 1

8 Hillmann
b.
p.
m.
p.
d.
p.

9
b.
p.
d.
p.

4 Jacob Hillmann [283]
b.
p.
m.
p.
d.
p.

10
b.
p.
m.
p.
d.
p.

5
b.
p.
d.
p.

11
b.
p.
d.
p.

2 Carl Friedrich Christian Hillmann
c. 2 Jan 1768 [280]
p. Galenbeck, Mecklenburg-Schwerin
m. 31 Oct 1799 [282]
p. Galenbeck, Mecklenburg-Schwerin
d. 9 Sep 1829
p. Kastorf, Mecklenburg-Schwerin

1 Johanna Sophia Elisabeth Hillmann
b. 31 May 1811 [133]
p. Galenbeck, Mecklenburg-Schwerin
m. about 1836 [132]
p.
d. 16 Dec 1903 [135]
p. Michigan City, LaPorte, Indiana
sp. Johann Carl Friedrich Theodor Wolf

12
b.
p.
m.
p.
d.
p.

6 Johann Westphal
b.
p.
m.
p.
d.
p.

13
b.
p.
d.
p.

3 Christine Sophia Westphal
b. about 1781 [136]
p. Schwandt, Mecklenburg-Schwerin
d.
p.

14
b.
p.
m.
p.
d.
p.

7
b.
p.
d.
p.

15
b.
p.
d.
p.

Ancestor Chart

No. 1 on this chart is the same as no. 8 on chart no. 2

8
b.
p.
m.
p.
d.
p.

4
b.
p.
m.
p.
d.
p.

9
b.
p.
d.
p.

2 Hans Hinrich Weidemann [1]
b. circa 1680 [1]
p.
m. before 1714 [1]
p. Gemeinde Altenkrempe, Holstein
d.
p.

10
b.
p.
m.
p.
d.
p.

5
b.
p.
d.
p.

11
b.
p.
d.
p.

1 Hans Hinrich Weidemann [1]
b. about 1714 [1]
p. Kassau, Holstein
m. 6 Nov 1746 [1]
p. Altenkrempe, Holstein
d. 11 Jan 1798 [1]
p. Stolpe, Holstein
sp. Maria Elisabeth Schumacher[1]

12
b.
p.
m.
p.
d.
p.

6 Hans Muuß [286]
b. Est 1655 [287]
p.
m. 25 Aug 1678 [287]
p. Süsel, Holstein
d.
p.

13
b.
p.
d.
p.

3 Engel Muuß [284]
c. 25 Jul 1680 [285]
p. Süsel, Holstein
d.
p.

14
b.
p.
m.
p.
d.
p.

7 Margreth Bück [287]
b.
p.
d.
p.

15
b.
p.
d.
p.

Ancestor Chart

No. 1 on this chart is the same as no. 9 on chart no. 2

```
                                                              8 _____
                                                              b.
                                                              p.
                                                              m.
                                  4 _____          p.
                                  b.                           d.
                                  p.                           p.
                                  m.                           9 _____
                                  p.                           b.
                                  d.                           p.
                                  p.                           d.
      2 Jochen Schumacher 1                                    p.
      b. Est 1680 1
      p.
      m.
      p.                                                       10 _____
      d.                                                       b.
      p.                                                       p.
                                                              m.
                                  5 _____          p.
                                  b.                           d.
                                  p.                           p.
                                  d.                           11 _____
                                  p.                           b.
                                                              p.
  1 Maria Elisabeth Schumacher 1                               d.
  b. about 1715 1                                              p.
  p. Sierhagen, Holstein
  m. 6 Nov 1746 1
  p. Altenkrempe, Holstein
  d. 25 Apr 1792 1                                             12 _____
  p. Stolpe, Holstein                                         b.
  sp. Hans Hinrich Weidemann1                                 p.
                                                              m.
                                  6 _____          p.
                                  b.                           d.
                                  p.                           p.
                                  m.                           13 _____
                                  p.                           b.
                                  d.                           p.
                                  p.                           d.
                                                              p.
      3 Sophia 1
      b. Est 1680 1
      p.
      d.                                                       14 _____
      p.                                                       b.
                                                              p.
                                                              m.
                                  7 _____          p.
                                  b.                           d.
                                  p.                           p.
                                  d.                           15 _____
                                  p.                           b.
                                                              p.
                                                              d.
                                                              p.
```

Ancestor Chart

No. 1 on this chart is the same as no. 11 on chart no. 2

8 _____
b.
p.
m.
p.
d.
p.

4 _____
b.
p.
m.
p.
d.
p.

9 _____
b.
p.
d.
p.

2 _____
b.
p.
m.
p.
d.
p.

10 _____
b.
p.
m.
p.
d.
p.

5 _____
b.
p.
d.
p.

11 _____
b.
p.
d.
p.

1 **Hedwig Wehde**[1] _____
b.
p.
m.
p.
d.
p.
sp. Hinrich Schumacher[1]

12 _____
b.
p.
m.
p.
d.
p.

6 _____
b.
p.
m.
p.
d.
p.

13 _____
b.
p.
d.
p.

3 _____
b.
p.
d.
p.

14 _____
b.
p.
m.
p.
d.
p.

7 _____
b.
p.
d.
p.

15 _____
b.
p.
d.
p.

Ancestor Report for Alma Marie Weidemann

First Generation

1. Alma Marie Weidemann, daughter of **Oscar Christian Weidemann** and **Mary E. Moynahan,** was born on 19 Apr 1904 in Erie, Erie, Pennsylvania,[108] was christened on 23 Jul 1904 in St. Andrew's Catholic Church, Erie, Erie, Pennsylvania,[109] died on 26 Aug 2004 in Ann Arbor, Washtenaw, Michigan,[110] and was buried in Woodlawn Cemetery, Detroit, Wayne, Michigan.

Christening Notes: Ann Sullivan was godmother at baptism

General Notes: Alma Marie Weidemann was born in Erie, Pennsylvania. She was baptized in St Andrew's Catholic Church, Erie, Pennsylvania 23 July 1904 as the "child of Oscar Weidemann and Maria E. Monahan." She moved to Detroit with her parents at an early age. Orphaned at age 15 as a result of a murder-suicide, she then lived with her aunt Alma in Detroit. She graduated from Michigan Normal School (now Eastern Michigan University, Ypsilanti, Michigan). She taught physical education in the Detroit Public Schools. She married Ewald Swanson in 1928. She worked for the state of Michigan in the 1960s and 1970s as a visual and hearing screener in the public schools. She lived in Vassar, Michigan until 2001.

Noted events in her life were:
- Resided: 1910, Detroit, Wayne, Michigan.[16]

- Residence: with her aunt Alma Weidemann, 1920-1923, Detroit, Wayne, Michigan.[111]

- Orphaned: 9 Feb 1920, Detroit, Wayne, Michigan.[112]

- Graduation: Michigan State Normal School (Eastern Michigan University), about 1926, Ypsilanti, Washtenaw, Michigan.

- Occupation: a physical education teacher at Webster School, 1928, Detroit, Wayne, Michigan.[113]

- Resided: 1930, Detroit, Wayne, Michigan.[44]

- Resided: 1935-1993, Vassar, Tuscola, Michigan.[114]

- Obituary: Vassar Pioneer Times, Sep 2004, Vassar, Tuscola, Michigan.[115]

   Alma Swanson of Ann Arbor, and formerly of Vassar, died on Thursday, August 26, 2004, in Ann Arbor. She was 100 years of age. She was born in Erie, Pennsylvania, the daughter of Oscar and Mary (Moynihan) Weidemann. Her husband, Dr. E. C. Swanson, preceded her in death.
   Mrs. Swanson is survived by three children, Shirley Smith, of St. Charles, Illinois, Richard (Jo) Swanson of Newland, North Carolina, and Margery (Jay) Haite of Ann Arbor; nine grandchildren; and seven great grandchildren.
   A family burial will take place in Detroit at Woodlawn Cemetery.
   Those planning an expression of sympathy may wish to consider the Bullard Sanford Memorial Library of Vassar or a memorial of choice.

- Obituary: Vassar Pioneer Times, as a letter to the editor by Buck Service, Sep 2004.

   Another era in Vassar history has just passed. Mrs. Alma Swanson at 100 years of age has gone to her heavenly reward.
   For decades the Swanson family set a standard for the people of Vassar and Mrs. Swanson was quietly elegant. In all the years I have known her, she was always calm and unflappable.
   She raised her three children, Shirley, Richard and Margie to remain quiet, studious, and

Ancestor Report

ambitious. The only member of the family that was beyond her control was her husband, "Doc" E.C. Swanson. He was as outgoing as she was quiet.

Mrs. Swanson even bore a striking resemblance to the movie star Gloria Swanson, although there was never an actual connection between the two women.

In recent years she lived alone at her home on North Main Street in Vassar and only moved in with her daughter Shirley when she was no longer able to drive. More recently she moved in with her daughter, Margie, in Ann Arbor, and it was there she spent her last days.

Although gone, her memory still lives in the minds of all who knew her. She was perhaps the last of the old guard in Vassar. The changing of the century and the millennium signalled a time for the slow change of a new society. Will we have a new Alma Swanson to help us set our sights high? She was a grand lady the likes of which we will never see again.

Alma married **Ewald Conrad Swanson M. D.,** son of **Mickel Mickelsson Svens**[116] and **Clara Fredrika Spångberg,** on 22 Jan 1928 in Detroit, Wayne, Michigan. Ewald was born on 3 Jan 1900 in Au Train, Alger, Michigan,[117] died on 26 Sep 1987 in Saginaw, Saginaw, Michigan,[117] and was buried in Woodlawn Cemetery, Detroit, Wayne, Michigan. Another name for Ewald was Dib Swanson.

General Notes: Dr. Ewald C. Swanson graduated from Alma College in central Michigan in 1923 and worked as a woodworker for Ford Motor Co. in Detroit. After working in the medical department at Ford he entered Wayne State University College of Medicine. He interned at Receiving Hospital, Detroit, and became house physician at Wyandotte General Hospital. In 1932 he moved to Vassar, Michigan, and took over the practice of Dr. W. A. Wellmeyer. He was executive secretary of the Michigan State Medical Society. He maintained a summer home in Greenbush, Michigan, on Lake Huron.

Noted events in his life were:
- Resided: 1900, Au Train, Alger, Michigan.[14]
- Resided: 1910, McMillan, Luce, Michigan.[16]
- Graduation: Newberry High School, 1918, Newberry, Luce, Michigan.
- Occupation: die repairman at auto factory, 1920, Detroit, Wayne, Michigan.[44]
- Occupation: medic in an automobile factory, 1924, Detroit, Wayne, Michigan.
- Graduation: Alma College, 1923, Alma, Gratiot, Michigan.
- Resided: 1930, Detroit, Wayne, Michigan.[44]
- Occupation: medical attendant at auto plant, 1930, Detroit, Wayne, Michigan.[44]
- Graduation: Wayne State University Medical School, 1931, Detroit, Wayne, Michigan.[118]
- Occupation: physician, 1932, Vassar, Tuscola, Michigan.
- Property: summer cottage, after 1940, Greenbush, Alcona, Michigan.
- Event: visited by August Spangberg, 1955, Newberry, Luce, Michigan.[119] August Spångberg, Swedish member of parliament, visited his relatives in Newberry. Ewald took time off from his medical practice to escort August on his trip. Ewald was August's first cousin.
- Organizations: Executive Secretary of the Michigan State Board of Registration, between 1956 and 1967.
- Elected: President of the Federation of State Medical Boards of the United States, 1963.
- Fact: Y-DNA test. Ewald's Y-DNA (via a test of Michael Swanson) shows his patrilineal

ancestors were in haplotype N1c1. Approximately 60% of all Finns are in this haplogroup, and its earliest ancestors originated in Southern Siberia circa 10,000 years ago and migrated to Finland circa 5000 years ago.

Ancestor Report

Second Generation (Parents)

2. Oscar Christian Weidemann, son of **Christian Heinrich Johannes Weidemann**[1] and **Maria Sophia Caroline Christine Wolf,** was born on 1 Aug 1871 in Detroit, Wayne, Michigan,[31] died on 9 Feb 1920 in Detroit, Wayne, Michigan,[26] and was buried on 12 Feb 1920 in Woodlawn Cemetery, Detroit, Wayne, Michigan.[4]

General Notes: Oscar grew up in Detroit. He studied art in New York and won a scholarship for a year at the Royal Academy of Art in Berlin. He started a decorating business in Erie, Pennsylvania about 1901. He and his wife moved to Detroit about 1905 where he worked with his father as a painter.

Noted events in his life were:

• Resided: at 44 Croghan (Monroe), 1880, Detroit, Wayne, Michigan.[12]

• Education: completed 8th grade at Washington School (Detroit Public Schools), 24 Jun 1887, Detroit, Wayne, Michigan.[92] Admitted to Detroit High School.

• Education: studying art, about 1891-1893, New York.[93]

• Occupation: painter living with his father, 1891, Detroit, Wayne, Michigan.[94]

• Event: applied for a passport, 10 Oct 1893, New York, New York, New York.[95]

• Arrival: about Nov 1893, Hamburg.[96]

• Arrival: from Hamberg, 6 Nov 1893, Berlin, Germany.[96]

• Education: attended Königliche Kunstschule zu Berlin (Royal Art School in Berlin), about 11 Nov 1893-Nov 1894, Berlin, Germany.[97] Now part of the University of the Arts Berlin.

• Travel: travels to several cities, Jun 1894-Aug 1894, Germany.[96]

• Travel: visits his father's hometown, 6 Aug 1894 to 8 Aug 1894, Neustadt, Schleswig-Holstein, Germany.[96] His sketch of a home at Waschgraben 27 may indicate that his father or a relative lived there.

• Newspaper Article: Detroit Free Press, 30 Sep 1894.[97]

    Among the seventy-nine pupils who attended the Royal School of Art at Berlin during the last semester, nineteen passed the examination. Oscar C. Weidemann of Detroit was one of these, and was also awarded a premium. After studying several years in New York, Mr. Weidemann went to Europe, where he intends to complete his art studies.

• Departure: 17 Feb 1895, Hamburg.[98] on the *SS Russia*

• Arrival: 4 Mar 1895, New York, New York, New York.[9] from Hamburg on the *SS Russia* after a year abroad studying art.

• Residence: 141 W 13th street next door to Anna Sullivan (godmother of his child), before 1900-1901, Erie, Erie, Pennsylvania.[99]

• Residence: 1016 W. 6th (home), 710 State (office in 1903), 1902-1904, Erie, Erie, Pennsylvania.[100]

• Occupation: decorator residing at 1394 Belvidere, 1910, Detroit, Wayne, Michigan.[16]

• Occupation: painter residing at 1394 Belvidere, 1915, Detroit, Wayne, Michigan.[37]

- Occupation: painter in a paint shop residing at at 1394 Belvidere, 1920, Detroit, Wayne, Michigan.[24]

- Cause of death: from The Detroit News, 9 Feb 1920, Detroit, Wayne, Michigan.[101]

Girl Hears Shots Finds Dying Parents

Oscar Weidemann, 1294 Belvidere avenue, shot his wife Mary and then turned his revolver on himself, Sunday night, inflicting the wounds of which both died early today at Receiving Hospital. Their daughter, 17 years old, heard the shots and running from a bedroom saw their bodies lying on the floor. She rushed screaming to neighbors, who notified police.

Weidemann is believed to have been demented. He left a letter accusing his wife, his mother, his relatives and neighbors generally, and describing quarrels. The letter said he had been in Receiving Hospital for alcoholism.

According to Mrs. Eleanor Neville, next door, they heard the two shots and turned out the lights, fearing he might fire through their windows. Neighbors describe Mrs. Weidemann as a charming woman of 38, crippled, so she could seldom leave the house. They said that Weidemann was jealous, never allowing his wife or daughter to associate with neighbors or, even if he could help it, to walk up Gratiot avenue.

Weidemann's letter indicated he had furious quarrels with neighbors over rabbits and chickens invading his yard.

The daughter is being cared for by her grandmother, Mrs. Mary Weidemann, who is in serious condition as a result of a fall sustained a week ago.

- Cause of death: from The Detroit Free Press, 10 Feb 1920, Detroit, Wayne, Michigan.[102]

Woman Murdered by Husband who Turns Gun on Himself

Oscar Weideman, dying, Found with Pistol in Hand

A double shooting, in which Mrs. Mary Weideman, of 1394 Bevidere avenue, was killed by her husband, Oscar, who then turned the weapon on himslf, inflicting what is believed to be a mortal wound.

According to the story told to the police by Alma Weideman, daughter of the principals in the shooting affair, she had gone to bed and her mother was following her, when she heard something on the stairway outside her room. She hurried out and found her mother on the floor at the foot of the steps. He father lay a short distance away, clasping a pistol in his hand. Both were shot though the head. When the police arrived they found another pistol in Weideman's top pocket.

Believed to be Demented

The pair were taken to the Receiving hospital where Mrs. Weideman died at an early hour this morning. Mr. Weideman was not expected to live.

Police believe that Weideman was demented. He is said to have undergone treatment some years ago for mental trouble.

- Memoriam: Sep 1922.[103] $50 donation made in his honor to *The Painter and Decorator* journal.

Oscar married **Mary E. Moynahan** on 19 May 1901 in Buffalo, Erie, New York.[32] Mary was born on 24 Aug 1876 in New York,[104] died on 9 Feb 1920 in Detroit, Wayne, Michigan,[105] and was buried on 12 Feb 1920 in Woodlawn Cemetery, Detroit, Wayne, Michigan.[105]

The child from this marriage was:

    1   i.   **Alma Marie Weidemann** (born on 19 Apr 1904 in Erie, Erie, Pennsylvania - died on

Ancestor Report

26 Aug 2004 in Ann Arbor, Washtenaw, Michigan). Alma married **Ewald Conrad Swanson M. D.,** son of **Mickel Mickelsson Svens**[116] and **Clara Fredrika Spångberg,** on 22 Jan 1928 in Detroit, Wayne, Michigan. Ewald was born on 3 Jan 1900 in Au Train, Alger, Michigan,[117] died on 26 Sep 1987 in Saginaw, Saginaw, Michigan,[117] and was buried in Woodlawn Cemetery, Detroit, Wayne, Michigan. Another name for Ewald was Dib Swanson.

3. Mary E. Moynahan, daughter of **John Minahan**[32] and **Mary O'Brien**,[32] was born on 24 Aug 1876 in New York,[104] died on 9 Feb 1920 in Detroit, Wayne, Michigan,[105] and was buried on 12 Feb 1920 in Woodlawn Cemetery, Detroit, Wayne, Michigan.[105]

Christening Notes: Ann Sullivan was godmother at baptism.

General Notes:
   Mary claims in her marriage license that she was born in New York City, New York, but more likely she was born in nearby Westchester County, New York. She was disabled, perhaps having a club foot.
   She is listed as Mary E. Lardner in the 1880 Albany census, in the same home as her widowed father John Moynahan and her siblings. According to the Albany city archives, Mrs. Lardner had only one daughter, Anne, so Mary. E. Larner was Mary E. Moynahan. After her father left Albany, she stayed with the McNamara family.
   It is not known how Oscar and Mary first met, but they were married in Buffalo, New York in 1901. After their daughter, Alma, was born in Erie in 1904, they moved to Detroit in 1905 where Oscar worked as a painter with his father.
   In 1920, Mary was murdered by her husband.[49]

Noted events in her life were:
• Religion: Roman Catholic.

• Resided: 1880, Albany, Albany, New York.[12]

• Resided: with William and Emma McNamara, 1892, Albany, Albany, New York.[106] Mary does not appear with them in the 1900 census.

• Resided: after May 1901, Erie, Erie, Pennsylvania.[32]

• Resided: at 1394 Belvidere, 1910, Detroit, Wayne, Michigan.[16]

• Resided: at 1394 Belvidere, 1920, Detroit, Wayne, Michigan.[24]

• Cause of death: by murder, shot by her husband., 9 Feb 1920, Detroit, Wayne, Michigan.[107]

Mary married **Oscar Christian Weidemann** on 19 May 1901 in Buffalo, Erie, New York.[32] Oscar was born on 1 Aug 1871 in Detroit, Wayne, Michigan,[31] died on 9 Feb 1920 in Detroit, Wayne, Michigan,[26] and was buried on 12 Feb 1920 in Woodlawn Cemetery, Detroit, Wayne, Michigan.[4]

Ancestor Report

Third Generation (Grandparents)

4. Christian Heinrich Johannes Weidemann,[1] son of **Claus Friederich Weidemann**[1] and **Anna Catherina Hedewig Ahrend**,[1] was born on 26 Feb 1837 in Neustadt, Ostholstein, Holstein,[2] died on 22 Jun 1913 in Detroit, Wayne, Michigan,[3] and was buried on 25 Jun 1913 in Woodlawn Cemetery, Detroit, Wayne, Michigan.[4] The cause of his death was apoplexy.

> General Notes: Born in Neustadt in Holstein, he lived in Austria before coming to America in 1866 with his brother. He worked for Wright and Company, a nationally-known design firm, which provided interior design and architecture services for large homes, commercial buildings, and government buildings. He worked as a fresco painter and supervised large projects including the interior decoration of the Michigan capitol building.

Noted events in his life were:
- Resided: on Waschgraben, circa 1846, Neustadt, Ostholstein, Holstein.[5] The family probably resided on Waschgraben, which is east of the church in the 3rd quarter. Oscar Weidemann made a sketch of the house when he visited Neustadt in 1894.

- Resided: about 1860, Vienna, Austria.[6]

- Occupation: painter, before 1866, Hamburg.[7]

- Emigration: 15 May 1866, Hamburg.[8] on the bark *Apollo* with his brother Henry

- Immigration: 6 Jul 1866, New York, New York, New York.[9] on the *Apollo*

- Occupation: fresco painter, 1870, Detroit, Wayne, Michigan.[10]

- Occupation: fresco painter, 1877, Detroit, Wayne, Michigan.[11]

- Occupation: fresco painter residing downtown at 44 Croghan (Monroe) near Cadillac Square, 1880, Detroit, Wayne, Michigan.[12]

- Occupation: decorating supervisor with William Wright Co. at the state capitol building, about 1888-1889, Lansing, Ingham, Michigan.[13]

- Occupation: decorator, 1900, Detroit, Wayne, Michigan.[14]

- Home Built: from The Detroit Free Press, 16 Apr 1905, Detroit, Wayne, Michigan.[15]

  Architects Norval Wardrop and Louis Keil have prepared plans and have let contracts for a residence for Christian Weidemann, on the north side of Erskine street, between John R. and Brush streets. It is to be a solid paving brick house, slate roof, galvanized cornice, hardwood finish for the interior and hardwood floors in the principal rooms, hot water for heating, combination lighting, mantels and modern sanitary plumbing. The dimensions are 32x50. The following contracts have been awarded: Mason work, LeMay & Whelun; carpenter, George Watt; plumbing and heating, John F. Jones; plastering, Gustay Jahnke; painting, William Wright Co.

- Occupation: master painter, 1910, Detroit, Wayne, Michigan.[16]

- Resided: 93 Erskine, 1913, Detroit, Wayne, Michigan.[17]

- Cause of death: apoplexy, 22 Jun 1913.[4]

- Obituary: from the Detroit Free Press, 23 Jun 1913.[18]

Ancestor Report

Christian Weidemann, Aged Designer, Dies
Succumbs to Heart Disease Sunday Monday at his Detroit Home.
Christian Weideman, 75 years old, for more than 40 years connected with the firm of William Wright & Co., as a designer, dies suddenly early Sunday morning at his home, 93 Erskine street, of heart disease.

Mr. Weideman was in his usual health when he retired Saturday night but complained about 2:30 a. m. of being ill and later died.

Mr. Weideman, along with work on other public buildings, superintended the decoration of the state capitol at Lansing about 20 years ago.

The funeral will be held Wednesday at 2 p. m. from the house and burial will be private.

Mr. Weideman was born in Neustadt, Germany, in 1837, and came to Detroit about 45 years ago. His first employment in Detroit was with William Wright and he continued with him until his death. As the firm went through various changes in ownership, management and name, Mr. Weideman acquired a financial interest.

He is survived by a widow and seven children, Oscar, Mathilde, assistant principal of the Detroit Normal School, Alma Caroline, Emma, Walter and Mrs. E. Von der Heide.

Christian married **Maria Sophia Caroline Christine Wolf** on 6 Feb 1868 in Detroit, Wayne, Michigan.[19] Maria was born on 3 Aug 1841 in Wolkow, Wildberg, Pommern, Preußen,[20] was christened on 12 Sep 1841 in Wolkow, Wildberg, Pommern, Preußen,[21] and died on 14 Mar 1928 in Detroit, Wayne, Michigan.[22] Another name for Maria was Mary Wolff.

Children from this marriage were:

 i. **Henry Weidemann**[26] was born on 9 Nov 1868 in Detroit, Wayne, Michigan,[27] died on 10 Aug 1869 in Detroit, Wayne, Michigan,[27] and was buried in Woodlawn Cemetery, Detroit, Wayne, Michigan.

 ii. **Laura F. Weidemann**[26] was born on 13 Dec 1869 in Detroit, Wayne, Michigan[28] and died on 21 Dec 1941 in Detroit, Wayne, Michigan.[29] Laura married **Edmund Christian von der Heide**,[26] son of **Christian von der Heide**[83] and **Wilhelmina Backhaus**,[83] on 28 Jun 1899 in Detroit, Wayne, Michigan.[30] Edmund was born on 22 Dec 1861 in Detroit, Wayne, Michigan[84] and died on 25 Jun 1943 in Eloise, Wayne, Michigan.[29]

2 iii. **Oscar Christian Weidemann** (born on 1 Aug 1871 in Detroit, Wayne, Michigan - died on 9 Feb 1920 in Detroit, Wayne, Michigan). Oscar married **Mary E. Moynahan,** daughter of **John Minahan**[32] and **Mary O'Brien**,[32] on 19 May 1901 in Buffalo, Erie, New York.[32] Mary was born on 24 Aug 1876 in New York,[104] died on 9 Feb 1920 in Detroit, Wayne, Michigan,[105] and was buried on 12 Feb 1920 in Woodlawn Cemetery, Detroit, Wayne, Michigan.[105]

 iv. **Mathilda "Tilly" Weidemann**[26] was born on 16 Dec 1875 in Detroit, Wayne, Michigan[33] and died on 15 Feb 1961 in Detroit, Wayne, Michigan.[34]

 v. **Alma Weidemann**[26] was born on 1 Oct 1876 in Detroit, Wayne, Michigan[47] and died on 4 Jan 1928 in Detroit, Wayne, Michigan.[26]

 vi. **Sarah Weidemann** was born on 3 Jul 1878 in Detroit, Wayne, Michigan.[50]

 vii. **Caroline "Carrie" Weidemann** was born on 23 Jul 1880 in Detroit, Wayne, Michigan[51] and died on 29 Nov 1962.[26] Caroline married **George Johannes Dingeldey**,[54] son of **Johann Phillipp Dingeldey** and **Mary Hasselbach,** on 25 Jan 1936.[26] George was born on 28 May 1862 in Buffalo, Erie, New York,[55] died on 24 Dec 1939 in Wayne, Wayne, Michigan,[55] and was buried in Canton, Wayne,

Michigan.[56]

viii. **Emma Weidemann**[26] was born on 12 Jan 1883 in Detroit, Wayne, Michigan[59] and died on 27 Jul 1964.[26]

ix. **Walter Weidemann**[62] was born on 23 Jul 1885 in Detroit, Wayne, Michigan,[63] was christened on 24 Apr 1886 in Wayne, Michigan,[64] died on 2 Jun 1955 in Port Huron, St. Clair, Michigan,[65] and was buried in Woodlawn Cemetery, Detroit, Wayne, Michigan. Walter married **Laura Lichtenberg**,[26] daughter of **Christian J. Lichtenberg**[74] and **Caroline Wenzel**,[75] on 1 Jul 1914 in Detroit, Wayne, Michigan.[73] Laura was born on 6 Nov 1878 in Detroit, Wayne, Michigan[76] and died on 24 Oct 1947 in Detroit, Wayne, Michigan.[29] Walter next married **Clara Margaret Diem,** daughter of **Theobald Diem**[14] and **Mary Ann Krantz**,[78] on 4 Jan 1950 in St. Margaret Mary's Church, Detroit, Wayne, Michigan.[77] Clara was born on 24 May 1890 in Carsonville, Sanilac, Michigan,[79] died in Mar 1966 in Port Huron, St. Clair, Michigan,[80] and was buried in Woodlawn Cemetery, Detroit, Wayne, Michigan.

5. Maria Sophia Caroline Christine Wolf, daughter of **Johann Carl Friedrich Theodor "Carl" Wolf** and **Johanna Sophia Elisabeth "Elizabeth" Hillmann,** was born on 3 Aug 1841 in Wolkow, Wildberg, Pommern, Preußen,[20] was christened on 12 Sep 1841 in Wolkow, Wildberg, Pommern, Preußen,[21] and died on 14 Mar 1928 in Detroit, Wayne, Michigan.[22] Another name for Maria was Mary Wolff.

> Christening Notes: Sponsors were: 1. girl Christine Wolf, Schossow, 2. girl Sophie Wolf, Schossow, 3. girl Henriette Hillmann, Galenbeck, 4. wife Johanna Feul, Galenbeck, 5. Joachim Ehrenreich, Wolde, 6. Johann Sievert, Wolkow, 7. bricklayer Martin Tessin, Japzow.

Noted events in her life were:
- Emigration: 1 May 1858, Hamburg.[23] on the bark *Donau*.
- Immigration: 7 Jun 1858, New York, New York, New York.[9]
- Resided: at 44 Croghan (Monroe), 1880, Detroit, Wayne, Michigan.[12]
- Resided: 116 Monroe, 1900, Detroit, Wayne, Michigan.[14]
- Resided: 93 Erskine, 1910, Detroit, Wayne, Michigan.[16] 7 of 8 children living.
- Resided: 93 Erskine, 1920, Detroit, Wayne, Michigan.[24]
- Fact: Home renumbered from 93 to 269 Erskine, 1921, Detroit, Wayne, Michigan.[25]

Maria married **Christian Heinrich Johannes Weidemann**[1] on 6 Feb 1868 in Detroit, Wayne, Michigan.[19] Christian was born on 26 Feb 1837 in Neustadt, Ostholstein, Holstein,[2] died on 22 Jun 1913 in Detroit, Wayne, Michigan,[3] and was buried on 25 Jun 1913 in Woodlawn Cemetery, Detroit, Wayne, Michigan.[4] The cause of his death was apoplexy.

6. John Minahan[32] was born circa 1834 in Ireland.[223] Another name for John was John Moynahan.

Noted events in his life were:
- Religion: Roman Catholic.
- Resided: 1854, Croom, Limerick, Ireland.[224]
- Immigrated: to America, about 1866.[9] There is a John Minehan on the *SS City of New York* arriving in New York on 16 April 1866, however it is not proven that this is the same John

Ancestor Report

Minahan.

- Occupation: stonecutter, 1870, Eastchester, Westchester, New York. [10]
- Resided: about 1872, New York. [12]
- Occupation: stonecutter residing at 26 Grand, 1875, Hartford, Hartford, Connecticut. [37]
- Occupation: stonecutter residing at 27 Grand, 1876, Hartford, Hartford, Connecticut. [37]
- Citizenship: application filed, 13 Oct 1876, Yonkers, Westchester, New York.[225] Witnessed by Denis Murphy and John Murphy. Form originally filled out as Millihan, then crossed out and corrected to Moynihan. Signed with an X.
- Inmate: almshouse for two nights, 18 Nov 1876, Albany, Albany, New York.[226] "for want of labor."
- Occupation: stonecutter residing at 41 Chestnut, 1879, Albany, Albany, New York.[37]
- Occupation: stonecutter residing at 336 State St., 1880, Albany, Albany, New York.[227]
- Occupation: stonecutter residing at 47 High, 1883, Albany, Albany, New York.[37]
- Occupation: stonecutter residing at 85 Elk, 1885, Albany, Albany, New York.[37]
- Occupation: stonecutter residing at 2624 K NW, 1889, Washington, District of Columbia.[37] Lived with his son Michael.
- Occupation: stonecutter, 1891-1901, Cincinnati, Hamilton, Ohio.[24]

John married **Mary O'Brien**[32] on 8 Oct 1854 in St. Mary of the Assumption Church, Croom, Limerick, Ireland.[228] Mary was born circa 1834 in Limerick, Ireland,[229] died on 18 Jun 1879 in Albany, Albany, New York,[230] and was buried in St. Mary's, Albany, Albany, New York.[231] The cause of her death was carcinoma of uterus.

Marriage Notes: The witnesses to the marriage were Matthew Moloney and Mary Minahan. Fr. James O'Shea celebrated the wedding as curate of Croom parish.

Children from this marriage were:

i. **Michael E. Minahan** was born in Aug 1855 in Croom, Limerick, Ireland,[184] was christened on 26 Aug 1855 in St. Mary of the Assumption Church, Croom, Limerick, Ireland,[232] died on 3 Oct 1924 in Tarrytown, Westchester, New York,[233] and was buried in Sleepy Hollow Cemetery, Tarrytown, Westchester, New York.[234] Another name for Michael was Michael E. Moynahan. Michael married **Margaret McIntyre** about 1888.[14] Margaret was born in Aug 1863 in Ireland,[14] died on 5 Aug 1946, and was buried in Sleepy Hollow Cemetery, Tarrytown, Westchester, New York.

ii. **Patrick Minahan** was christened on 23 May 1857 in St. Mary of the Assumption Church, Croom, Limerick, Ireland[235] and died on 17 Oct 1935 in Manhattan, New York, New York.[236] Another name for Patrick was Patrick Moynahan.

iii. **Joseph Minahan** was christened on 1 Feb 1859 in St. Mary of the Assumption Church, Croom, Limerick, Ireland.[238]

iv. **Joseph Minahan** was christened on 8 Feb 1863 in St. Mary of the Assumption Church, Croom, Limerick, Ireland[239] and died on 19 Apr 1898 in Boston, Suffolk, Massachusetts.[240] Another name for Joseph was Joseph Moynahan.

v. **John Moynahan** was born about 1866.[241]

vi. **Thomas Francis Moynahan** was born on 29 Aug 1868 in Mt. Vernon, Westchester,

New York[10] and was christened on 6 Sep 1868 in Immaculate Conception Church, Tuckahoe, Westchester, New York.[242]

vii. **May Moynahan** was born in 1872 in New York.[12]

viii. **William S. Moynahan**[243] was born on 15 Aug 1873 in New York,[244] died on 4 Oct 1938 in Cleveland, Cuyahoga, Ohio,[243] and was buried on 7 Oct 1938 in Alger Cemetery, Cleveland, Cuyahoga, Ohio.[245] The cause of his death was Pulmonary tuberculosis. William married **Harriet Rose Jolly**,[253] daughter of **William Perry Jolly**[129] and **Harriet Catherine Selby**,[254] on 27 Dec 1902 in Marion, Grant, Indiana.[253] Harriet was born on 15 Aug 1859 in Alexandria, Campbell, Kentucky,[255] died on 7 May 1915 in Cincinnati, Hamilton, Ohio,[248] and was buried in Greenlawn Cemetery, Newport, Campbell, Kentucky.[248] William next married **Anna Rainerman**,[256] daughter of **Bernard John Rainerman**[257] and **Harmke Bess**,[257] on 20 Dec 1915 in Franklin, Ohio.[257] Anna was born on 31 Mar 1880 in Amsterdam, Holland[257] and died on 23 Jun 1949 in Lakewood, Cuyahoga, Ohio.[258]

ix. **Edward T. Moynahan** was born on 27 Apr 1875 in Hartford, Hartford, Connecticut[259] and died on 12 Jun 1911 in Tewksbury, Middlesex, Massachusetts.[240] The cause of his death was chronic kidney disease.

3 x. **Mary E. Moynahan** (born on 24 Aug 1876 in New York - died on 9 Feb 1920 in Detroit, Wayne, Michigan). Mary married **Oscar Christian Weidemann,** son of **Christian Heinrich Johannes Weidemann**[1] and **Maria Sophia Caroline Christine Wolf,** on 19 May 1901 in Buffalo, Erie, New York.[32] Oscar was born on 1 Aug 1871 in Detroit, Wayne, Michigan,[31] died on 9 Feb 1920 in Detroit, Wayne, Michigan,[26] and was buried on 12 Feb 1920 in Woodlawn Cemetery, Detroit, Wayne, Michigan.[4]

7. Mary O'Brien[32] was born circa 1834 in Limerick, Ireland,[229] died on 18 Jun 1879 in Albany, Albany, New York,[230] and was buried in St. Mary's, Albany, Albany, New York.[231] The cause of her death was carcinoma of uterus.

Death Notes: 44 Chestnut Street in Albany, New York.

Burial Notes: She was probably removed to another cemetery when St. Mary's was closed. The land is now a high school.

Noted events in her life were:
• Religion: Roman Catholic.

• Immigrated: to America, Est 1866.

• Travel: 16 Jul 1868, New York.[9] on *SS Virginia* from Ireland

• Travel: 7 Sep 1869, New York, New York.[9] Returns to New York on the ship *SS Virginia* after a visit to Ireland.

• Resided: 1870, Eastchester, Westchester, New York.[10]

Mary married **John Minahan**[32] on 8 Oct 1854 in St. Mary of the Assumption Church, Croom, Limerick, Ireland.[228] John was born circa 1834 in Ireland.[223] Another name for John was John Moynahan.

Ancestor Report

Fourth Generation (Great-Grandparents)

8. Claus Friederich Weidemann,[1] son of **Claus Hinrich Weidemann**[1] and **Anna Elsabe Dorothea Haack,**[1] was born on 10 Dec 1801 in Stolpe, Ostholstein, Holstein[265] and died on 9 Mar 1881 in Neustadt, Ostholstein, Holstein.[1]

> Birth Notes: Born on the Sierhagen estate.

> General Notes: He was born in Stolpe in Holstein. He moved to Neustadt and raised his family in the 3rd quarter, probably on Waschgraben. His wife died in 1846 making him a single father. He later moved in with a family in the 2nd quarter, probably on Kremper Street.

> Noted events in his life were:
> - Occupation: Laborer, 1860, Neustadt, Ostholstein, Holstein.[289] According to the 1860 census, Claus was living in the 3rd quarter, which lies southeast of the church within the city wall. He is a widower living with Joh. Aug. Schöning and his wife Anna Maria.
>
> - Occupation: laborer, 1864, Neustadt, Ostholstein, Holstein.[290] In 1864 he is a 63-year old widower living in the 2nd Quarter (probably on Kremper Street) with Christian and Dorothea Plambeck and their three children. His eldest son Jakob lived on Kremper Street, his daughter married, and his two other sons, Christian and Heinrich, lived outside Holstein.

Claus married **Anna Catherina Hedewig Ahrend**[1] on 21 Mar 1824 in Neustadt, Ostholstein, Holstein.[266] Anna was born in 1797 in Klenau, Grube, Ostholstein, Holstein[267] and died on 26 Jan 1846 in Neustadt, Ostholstein, Holstein.[1] Another name for Anna was Catherine Arndt.[291]

> Marriage Notes: Anna's parents were deceased at the time of her wedding.[1]

Children from this marriage were:

    i.   **Jakob Frederick Weidemann**[1] was born on 24 Jun 1824 in Neustadt, Ostholstein, Holstein[266] and died on 9 Oct 1865 in Neustadt, Ostholstein, Holstein.[1] Jakob married **Christine Dorothea Wentorf**[1] on 29 Mar 1853 in Neustadt, Ostholstein, Holstein.[1] Christine was born in 1829 in Eutin, Ostholstein, Holstein[1] and died in 1898.[292]

    ii.   **Catharina Ida Johanna Weidemann**[1] was born on 7 Feb 1826 in Neustadt, Ostholstein, Holstein[266] and died on 14 May 1886 in Altona, Hamburg.[293] Catharina married **Johann Heinrich Derlin**.[1]

    iii.   **Johann Hinrich Friedrich Weidemann**[1] was born on 27 Nov 1827 in Neustadt, Ostholstein, Holstein[266] and died on 5 Dec 1827 in Neustadt, Ostholstein, Holstein.[1]

    iv.   **Maria Elizabeth Johanna Weidemann**[1] was born on 29 May 1829 in Neustadt, Ostholstein, Holstein[294] and died in 1921 in Detroit, Wayne, Michigan.[295] Maria married **Henry C. Hensler**, son of **Carl Hensler**. Henry was born in 1831 in Preußen[12] and died on 28 Mar 1905 in Detroit, Wayne, Michigan.[296]

    v.   **Elisabeth Margaretha Henriette Weidemann**[1] was born on 6 Aug 1831 in Neustadt, Ostholstein, Holstein[266] and died on 6 Jan 1835 in Neustadt, Ostholstein, Holstein.[1]

    vi.   **Anna Luise Jette Weidemann**[1] was born on 17 Nov 1835 in Neustadt, Ostholstein, Holstein.[1] Anna married **Grönwoldt**.

    vii.   **Heinrich Nicolaus Carl Weidemann** was born on 17 Nov 1835 in Neustadt, Ostholstein, Holstein[1] and died on 8 Nov 1895 in Detroit, Wayne, Michigan. Another name for Heinrich was Henry N.C. Weidemann.

4   viii.   **Christian Heinrich Johannes Weidemann**[1] (born on 26 Feb 1837 in Neustadt, Ostholstein, Holstein - died on 22 Jun 1913 in Detroit, Wayne, Michigan). Christian married **Maria Sophia Caroline Christine Wolf,** daughter of **Johann Carl Friedrich Theodor "Carl" Wolf** and **Johanna Sophia Elisabeth "Elizabeth" Hillmann,** on 6 Feb 1868 in Detroit, Wayne, Michigan.[19] Maria was born on 3 Aug 1841 in Wolkow, Wildberg, Pommern, Preußen,[20] was christened on 12 Sep 1841 in Wolkow, Wildberg, Pommern, Preußen,[21] and died on 14 Mar 1928 in Detroit, Wayne, Michigan.[22] Another name for Maria was Mary Wolff.

9. Anna Catherina Hedewig Ahrend,[1] daughter of **Hans Jürgen Ahrend**[1] and **Margaretha Elisabeth Westphal,**[1] was born in 1797 in Klenau, Grube, Ostholstein, Holstein[267] and died on 26 Jan 1846 in Neustadt, Ostholstein, Holstein.[1] Another name for Anna was Catherine Arndt.[291]

Anna married **Claus Friederich Weidemann**[1] on 21 Mar 1824 in Neustadt, Ostholstein, Holstein.[266] Claus was born on 10 Dec 1801 in Stolpe, Ostholstein, Holstein[265] and died on 9 Mar 1881 in Neustadt, Ostholstein, Holstein.[1]

10. Johann Carl Friedrich Theodor "Carl" Wolf, son of **Carl Friedrich Wolf**[120] and **Christina Dorothea Elisabeth Teage,**[121] was born on 7 Dec 1814 in Zwiedorf, Röckwitz, Mecklenburg-Schwerin,[122] was christened on 11 Dec 1814 in Röckwitz, Mecklenburg-Schwerin,[123] died on 20 Mar 1906 in Michigan City, LaPorte, Indiana,[124] and was buried in Greenwood Cemetery, Michigan City, LaPorte, Indiana.[56] Other names for Johann were Carl Wolff, Charles Wolff, and Karl Wolff.

Christening Notes: Sponsors were Anna Dorothea Friederica, wife of farmer Drews; Johann Friedrich Peters, farmhand in Zwiedorf; Carl Koepke, daylaborer in Zwiedorf.

General Notes: His last address before emigrating was Wildberg, Pomerania. He was educated to the age of fourteen, then apprenticed as a weaver. He brought his wife and eight children to America in 1858 on the sailing ship named *Donau* on a voyage that lasted five weeks. They immigrated through New York, New York and bought a tract of uncleared land fourteen miles west of Detroit where they built a log cabin. After farming the land for several years, they moved to the southwestern corner of Michigan in Berrien County where he bought an eighty acre farm in New Buffalo Township.[125]

Noted events in his life were:
• Confirmation: Lutheran church, 1829, Schossow, Altenhagen, Pommern, Preußen.[126]

• Occupation: weaver, 1841, Wolkow, Wildberg, Pommern, Preußen.[127]

• Occupation: weaver, 1844, Fouquettin, Wildberg, Pommern, Preußen.[127]

• Occupation: weaver, 1858, Wildberg, Wildberg, Pommern, Preußen.[9]

• Emigration: on the Donau, 1 May 1858, Hamburg.[23]

• Immigration: on the ship Donau, 7 Jun 1858, New York, New York, New York.[9]

• Warranty Deed Land: purchased 50 acres, 13 Jan 1859, Nankin, Wayne, Michigan.[128] Purchased land from Murenus Harrison and wife Augusta A. to Carl Wolf and John Conrad, recorded May 5 1860, for $1000 in section 24, Nankin. (The former farm is now a subdivision, and lies on the northeast corner of Middle Belt Road and Avondale Street.)

• Occupation: farmer, 1860, Nankin, Wayne, Michigan.[129]

• Mortgage Cancelled: 3 Aug 1863, Nankin, Wayne, Michigan.[128] The mortgage from Carl Wolff and John Conrad to Marenus Harrison, to Emily Harrison, to Joseph Dittmar, cancelled on face 3 Aug 1863 $200, section 24, Nankin.

- Warranty Deed Land: sold property, 11 Nov 1865, Nankin, Wayne, Michigan.[128] Land transferred from Carl Wolff, Elizabeth Wolff, and John Conrad to Charles Berrosnets (Bewernitz), $2000, section 24, Nankin.
- Occupation: farmer, 1870, New Buffalo, Berrien, Michigan.[10]
- Occupation: farmer, 1880, New Buffalo, Berrien, Michigan.[12]
- Farm: section 20, 80 acres, value $1580, 1892, New Buffalo, Berrien, Michigan.[130]
- Occupation: farmer, 1900, New Buffalo, Berrien, Michigan.[14]
- Obituary: Michigan City Dispatch, 22 Mar 1906.[131]

Karl Wolff died Tuesday at the home of his stepson, John Conrad, 312 East Seventh street, of paralysis. Mr. Wolff was stricken Monday morning, losing his voice and eyesight, and was unconscious until his death, which occurred at 10 o'clock Tuesday night.

Mr. Wolff was born in Prussia December 7, 1813, and was ninety-two years, three months and thirteen days old. In 1856 he came to this country, settling in Detroit, and from Detroit went to Berrien county, Michigan, where he lived on a farm until four years ago, when he retired and moved to Michigan City. He was married in the old country seventy years ago and his wife died here in 1903. Mr. Wolff leaves, besides the stepson at home with whom he died, three sons, two daughters, twenty-five grandchildren, and eleven great grand children. The children are Charles Wolff, Michigan City; Edmund Wolff, Deadwood, S.D., William Wolff, Miles City, Montana; Mrs. Chris Weidemann, Detroit; and Mrs. Peter Averly, Detroit. The funeral will be held at 2 o'clock Friday afternoon from the home of Charles Wolff at 1120 South Pine street, and the services will be conducted by the Rev. J.G. Hoch, pastor of St. John's Church.

Johann married **Johanna Sophia Elisabeth "Elizabeth" Hillmann** about 1836.[132] Johanna was born on 31 May 1811 in Galenbeck, Stavenhagen, Mecklenburg-Schwerin,[133] was christened on 3 Jun 1811 in Kastorf, Stavenhagen, Mecklenburg-Schwerin,[134] and died on 16 Dec 1903 in Michigan City, LaPorte, Indiana.[135] Another name for Johanna was Elizabeth Hillman.[136]

Marriage Notes: The marriage of Carl Wolf and Elisabeth Hillmann was probably in Kastorf, Stavenhagen.

Children from this marriage were:

    i.   **Carolina "Lena" Wolf** was born on 28 Mar 1839 in Pommern, Preußen,[139] died on 17 Aug 1904 in Canton, Wayne, Michigan,[140] and was buried in Glenwood Cemetery, Wayne, Wayne, Michigan. Another name for Carolina was Carolena Wolff. Carolina married **Carl Bewernitz** about 1857.[112] Carl was born on 22 Jun 1826 in Pommern, Preußen,[163] died on 14 May 1904 in Nankin, Wayne, Michigan,[164] and was buried in Glenwood Cemetery, Wayne, Wayne, Michigan. Other names for Carl were Carl Berrosnets and Charles Bewernitz.

5   ii.   **Maria Sophia Caroline Christine Wolf** (born on 3 Aug 1841 in Wolkow, Wildberg, Pommern, Preußen - died on 14 Mar 1928 in Detroit, Wayne, Michigan). Maria married **Christian Heinrich Johannes Weidemann**,[1] son of **Claus Friederich Weidemann**[1] and **Anna Catherina Hedewig Ahrend**,[1] on 6 Feb 1868 in Detroit, Wayne, Michigan.[19] Christian was born on 26 Feb 1837 in Neustadt, Ostholstein, Holstein,[2] died on 22 Jun 1913 in Detroit, Wayne, Michigan,[3] and was buried on 25 Jun 1913 in Woodlawn Cemetery, Detroit, Wayne, Michigan.[4] The cause of his death was apoplexy.

    iii.   **Auguste Friederike Caroline "Augusta" Wolf** was born on 5 Jan 1844 in

Fouquettin, Wildberg, Pommern, Preußen,[141] was christened on 28 Jan 1844 in Wildberg, Wildberg, Pommern, Preußen,[142] died on 21 Aug 1934,[56] and was buried in Woodmere Cemetery, Detroit, Wayne, Michigan.[56] Other names for Auguste were Fredricka Eberle and Augusta Wolff. Auguste married **Peter John Eberle** on 23 Dec 1863 in Detroit, Wayne, Michigan.[143] Peter was born on 21 Oct 1833 in Baden,[170] died on 17 Jul 1887,[56] and was buried in Woodmere Cemetery, Detroit, Wayne, Michigan.

iv.   **Friedrich Wilhelm Christian August Wolf** was born on 3 Feb 1846 in Fouquettin, Wildberg, Pommern, Preußen[144] and was christened on 7 Mar 1846 in Wildberg, Wildberg, Pommern, Preußen.[145]

v.   **Carl "Charles" Wolf** was born on 7 Feb 1847 in Pommern, Preußen,[146] died on 11 Jan 1924 in Michigan City, LaPorte, Indiana,[147] and was buried in Greenwood Cemetery, Michigan City, LaPorte, Indiana. Carl married **Caroline Magdalena Koch,** daughter of **Christian Koch** and **Catherine Lole,**[169] on 30 Oct 1877 in Romulus, Wayne, Michigan.[73] Caroline was born in 1855 in Romulus, Wayne, Michigan[73] and died about 1882.[125] Carl next married **Ida Cook,** daughter of **Charles Cook** and **Charlotte Westphal,** on 30 Mar 1884.[112] Ida was born on 9 Dec 1865 in Michigan City, LaPorte, Indiana,[187] died on 11 Mar 1947,[56] and was buried in Greenwood Cemetery, Michigan City, LaPorte, Indiana.[56]

vi.   **Wilhelm Friedrich Adolph "Edmund" Wolf**[148] was born on 26 Dec 1848 in Fouquettin, Wildberg, Pommern, Preußen,[149] was christened on 29 Dec 1848 in Wildberg, Wildberg, Pommern, Preußen,[150] died on 19 May 1934 in Detroit, Wayne, Michigan,[151] and was buried in Grand Lawn Cemetery, Detroit, Wayne, Michigan. Another name for Wilhelm was Edmund Wolff. Wilhelm married **Louise Sophie Koch,** daughter of **Felix Koch**[81] and **Louise Arnold,**[81] on 7 Mar 1882 in Detroit, Wayne, Michigan.[152] Louise was born on 27 Jan 1864 in Inkster, Wayne, Michigan.[14] Another name for Louise was Louise Sophie Wolff. Wilhelm next married **Esther "Et" Maria Bills,** daughter of **William Bills**[153] and **Julia Ann Bogue,** on 9 Jun 1894 in El Reno, Canadian, Oklahoma.[153] Esther was born on 25 Nov 1858 in Nankin, Wayne, Michigan,[209] died on 8 Nov 1933 in Detroit, Wayne, Michigan,[210] and was buried in Grand Lawn Cemetery, Detroit, Wayne, Michigan. Another name for Esther was Ester.

vii.   **Wilhelmine Sophie Caroline Dorothea "Emilie" Wolf** was born on 22 May 1852 in Fouquettin, Wildberg, Pommern, Preußen[154] and was christened on 26 Jun 1852 in Wildberg, Wildberg, Pommern, Preußen.[155]

viii.   **Johann Carl Friedrich Wilhelm "William Wallace" Wolf** was born on 19 Jul 1855 in Fouquettin, Wildberg, Pommern, Preußen,[156] was christened on 30 Jul 1855 in Wildberg, Wildberg, Pommern, Preußen,[157] died on 9 Mar 1934 in Miles City, Custer, Montana,[158] and was buried in Custer County Cemetery, Miles City, Custer, Montana.[56] Another name for Johann was William Wallace Wolff. Johann married **Lucille Perry,** daughter of **James S. Perry** and **Mary Jane Fries,** on 17 Feb 1892 in Mount Clemens, Macomb, Michigan.[159] Lucille was born on 27 Oct 1864 in Mount Clemens, Harrison, Macomb, Michigan[217] and died on 30 May 1951 in Billings, Yellowstone, Montana.[218] Another name for Lucille was Lucy Wolff. Johann next married **Rose Elizabeth Shannon,**[160] daughter of **John Shannon**[220] and **Mary Coffey,**[220] on 7 Dec 1929 in Big Timber, Sweet Grass, Montana.[161] Rose was born on 19 Oct 1886 in Preble, Fillmore, Minnesota[221] and died on 24 Nov 1966 in Miles City, Custer, Montana.[222]

11. Johanna Sophia Elisabeth "Elizabeth" Hillmann, daughter of **Carl Friedrich Christian Hillmann** and **Christine Sophia Westphal,** was born on 31 May 1811 in Galenbeck, Stavenhagen, Mecklenburg-Schwerin,[133] was christened on 3 Jun 1811 in Kastorf, Stavenhagen, Mecklenburg-Schwerin,[134] and died on 16 Dec 1903 in Michigan City, LaPorte, Indiana.[135] Another name for Johanna was Elizabeth Hillman.[136]

> Christening Notes: Sponsors were girl Catharina Friederica Gilow, Elisabeth Dorothea Rhoden, wife of worker Gottschalk, and worker Johann Joachim Matthies, all from Galenbeck.

Noted events in her life were:
- Emigration: 1 May 1858, Hamburg.[23] on the bark *Donau*
- Resided: 1860, Nankin, Wayne, Michigan.[129]
- Resided: 1870, New Buffalo, Berrien, Michigan.[10]
- Resided: 1880, New Buffalo, Berrien, Michigan.[12]
- Resided: 1900, New Buffalo, Berrien, Michigan.[14]
- Obituary: Michigan Dispatch, 17 Dec 1903.[137]

      Mrs. Wolff is survived by the following children: Mrs. Charles Bevernetz; Mrs. Chris Weideman and Mrs. Augusta Abrele, Detroit; John Conrad, a stepson, this city; Charles Wolff, Michigan City; Edmund Wolff, Deadwood, S.D.; William Wolff, Custer County, Montana.

- Obituary: Michigan City News, 23 Dec 1903.[138]

      Mrs. Elizabeth Wolff, wife of Carl Wolff, died at her home on East Seventh street at 7:30 o'clock Wednesday evening of old age. She was 92 years, 6 months and 17 days of age and had been sick less than two days. Deceased was a native of Germany, where she was born May 30, 1811. She was married in Germany, where she was bereaved of her husband, __ Conrad. She was later married to Mr. Wolff, the husband who now survives her. Mr. and Mrs. Wolff came to this country in 1858, locating in Detroit. In 1866 the family moved to New Buffalo, where they resided until 1901 -- when Mr. and Mrs. Wolff and a son moved to this city.
      Deceased was the mother of Charles Wolff, well-know resident of this city.
      Mrs. Wolff is survived by her husband and seven adult children. John Conrad, residing at home; Charles Wolff of this city; Edmund Wolff residing in South Dakota; William Wolff, living in Miles City, Montana; and three married daughters living in Detroit. One daughter preceded the mother to that home beyond.
      Funeral Saturday Afternoon at 2 o'clock, from the home of Charles Wolff, 1120 Pine street, Rev. J.G. Hoch officiating.

Johanna married **Christian Martin Conrad,** son of **Frederick Conrad,** on 7 Sep 1832 in Galenbeck, Stavenhagen, Mecklenburg-Schwerin.[297] Christian was born in 1784 in Rosenow, Stavenhagen, Pommern, Preußen[136] and died after 1833 in Galenbeck, Stavenhagen, Mecklenburg-Schwerin.

Noted events in his life were:
- Occupation: a blacksmith, 1819, Galenbeck, Stavenhagen, Mecklenburg-Schwerin.[136]
- Occupation: master smith, 1832, Galenbeck, Stavenhagen, Mecklenburg-Schwerin.[298]

Ancestor Report

The child from this marriage was:

  i. **Johann Carl Friedrich Conrad** was born on 25 Nov 1833 in Galenbeck, Stavenhagen, Mecklenburg-Schwerin,[299] was christened on 1 Dec 1833 in Kastorf, Stavenhagen, Mecklenburg-Schwerin,[299] and died on 24 Feb 1910 in Michigan City, LaPorte, Indiana.[300] Another name for Johann was John Conrad.

Johanna next married **Johann Carl Friedrich Theodor "Carl" Wolf** about 1836.[132] Johann was born on 7 Dec 1814 in Zwiedorf, Röckwitz, Mecklenburg-Schwerin,[122] was christened on 11 Dec 1814 in Röckwitz, Mecklenburg-Schwerin,[123] died on 20 Mar 1906 in Michigan City, LaPorte, Indiana,[124] and was buried in Greenwood Cemetery, Michigan City, LaPorte, Indiana.[56] Other names for Johann were Carl Wolff, Charles Wolff, and Karl Wolff.

Ancestor Report

Fifth Generation (Great Great-Grandparents)

16. Claus Hinrich Weidemann,[1] son of **Hans Hinrich Weidemann**[1] and **Anna Margaretha Schumacher**,[1] was born on 8 May 1780 in Stolpe, Ostholstein, Holstein[1] and died on 1 Dec 1857 in Kassau, Ostholstein, Holstein.[1]

Noted events in his life were:
- Occupation: farmhand (Dienstknecht), 1803, Kassau, Ostholstein, Holstein.[301]

- Occupation: laborer (Arbeitsmann), after 1803, Kassau, Ostholstein, Holstein.[1]

- Cause of death: weakness of old age, 1857.[1]

Claus married **Anna Elsabe Dorothea Haack**[1] on 11 Oct 1800 in Altenkrempe, Ostholstein, Holstein.[1] Anna was born on 30 Jun 1777 in Kassau, Ostholstein, Holstein[1] and died on 2 Feb 1855 in Kassau, Ostholstein, Holstein.[1]

Children from this marriage were:

8   i.   **Claus Friederich Weidemann**[1] (born on 10 Dec 1801 in Stolpe, Ostholstein, Holstein - died on 9 Mar 1881 in Neustadt, Ostholstein, Holstein). Claus married **Anna Catherina Hedewig Ahrend**,[1] daughter of **Hans Jürgen Ahrend**[1] and **Margaretha Elisabeth Westphal**,[1] on 21 Mar 1824 in Neustadt, Ostholstein, Holstein.[266] Anna was born in 1797 in Klenau, Grube, Ostholstein, Holstein[267] and died on 26 Jan 1846 in Neustadt, Ostholstein, Holstein.[1] Another name for Anna was Catherine Arndt.[291]

       ii.   **Ida Lucia Weidemann**[1] was born on 21 Mar 1803 in Kassau, Ostholstein, Holstein[1] and died on 24 Mar 1860 in Stolpe, Ostholstein, Holstein.[1] Another name for Ida was Ida Catharina Weidemann.[1] Ida married **Wulf Peter Christian Stender**,[1] son of **Friedrich Adolph Stender**[1] and **Margaretha Magdalena Evers**,[1] on 25 Oct 1828 in Stolpe, Ostholstein, Holstein.[1] Wulf was born on 26 May 1802 in Kassau, Ostholstein, Holstein[1] and died on 8 May 1848 in Stolpe, Ostholstein, Holstein.[1]

      iii.   **Marcus Hinrich Wulf Weidemann**[1] was born on 8 Feb 1805 in Kassau, Ostholstein, Holstein[1] and died on 28 Apr 1844 in Kassau, Ostholstein, Holstein.[1] The cause of his death was tuberculosis.[1] Marcus married **Ida Wilhelmine Wede**,[1] daughter of **Wulf Hinrich Wede**[1] and **Elisabeth Dorothea Weidemann**,[1] on 21 Apr 1839 in Altenkrempe, Ostholstein, Holstein.[1] Another name for Ida was Ida Wilhelmine Weidemann.

      iv.   **Wulf Hinrich Weidemann**[1] was born on 28 Aug 1807 in Kassau, Ostholstein, Holstein[1] and died circa 1810 in Kassau, Ostholstein, Holstein.[1]

       v.   **Wulf Hinrich Weidemann**[1] was born on 6 Jun 1810 in Kassau, Ostholstein, Holstein[1] and died on 20 Jan 1812 in Kassau, Ostholstein, Holstein.[1]

      vi.   **Margretha Wilhelmine Weidemann**[1] was born on 14 Apr 1812 in Kassau, Ostholstein, Holstein[1] and died on 26 Jan 1867 in Eutin, Ostholstein, Holstein.[1] Margretha married **Christian Georg Koerner**,[1] son of **Johann Joachim Kerner**[1] and **Magdalena Dorothea Brey**,[1] on 13 Nov 1835 in Eutin, Ostholstein, Holstein.[1] Christian was born on 23 Aug 1811 in Eutin, Ostholstein, Holstein[1] and died on 22 May 1866 in Eutin, Ostholstein, Holstein.[1]

     vii.   **Magnus Peter Wulf Weidemann**[1] was born on 24 Nov 1814 in Kassau, Ostholstein, Holstein[302] and died on 15 May 1884 in Kassau, Ostholstein,

Holstein.[1] Magnus married **Anna Catherine Caroline Hein**,[1] daughter of **Carl Friedrich Hein**[1] and **Anna Elisabeth Knoop**,[1] on 26 Nov 1844 in Schönwalde, Ostholstein, Holstein.[302] Anna was born on 27 Mar 1821 in Langenhagen, Ostholstein, Holstein[1] and died on 18 Jun 1869 in Kassau, Ostholstein, Holstein.[1] The cause of her death was cancer of the stomach. Magnus next married **Elisabeth Dorothea Witt** on 29 Oct 1869 in Altenkrempe, Ostholstein, Holstein.[1]

viii.   **Ida Christina Henriette Weidemann**[303] was born on 9 Apr 1817 in Kassau, Ostholstein, Holstein.[1] Ida married **Johann Friedrich Kloth**,[1] son of **Johann Friedrich Kloth** and **Friederike Dorothea Schmueser**,[1] on 14 Dec 1838 in Altenkrempe, Ostholstein, Holstein.[1] Johann was born on 24 Apr 1808 in Griebel, Ostholstein, Holstein.[1] Another name for Johann was Fritz Kloth.

ix.   **Friederike Wilhelmine Weidemann**[1] was born on 18 Mar 1822 in Kassau, Ostholstein, Holstein[1] and died circa 1855.[1] Friederike had a relationship with **Friedrich Timm**.[1] This couple did not marry. Friedrich was born in Merendorf, Ostholstein, Holstein.[1]

17. Anna Elsabe Dorothea Haack,[1] daughter of **Hans Detlef Haack**[1] and **Anna Elsabe Diekmann**,[1] was born on 30 Jun 1777 in Kassau, Ostholstein, Holstein[1] and died on 2 Feb 1855 in Kassau, Ostholstein, Holstein.[1]

Anna married **Claus Hinrich Weidemann**[1] on 11 Oct 1800 in Altenkrempe, Ostholstein, Holstein.[1] Claus was born on 8 May 1780 in Stolpe, Ostholstein, Holstein[1] and died on 1 Dec 1857 in Kassau, Ostholstein, Holstein.[1]

18. Hans Jürgen Ahrend[1] was born in 1766.[268] Another name for Hans was Juergen Arndt.[1]

Noted events in his life were:
- Occupation: laborer, Klenau, Grube, Ostholstein, Holstein.[1]

- Occupation: 1803, Klenau, Grube, Ostholstein, Holstein.[268] He was the father of household and a laborer with land (Hausvater Inste mit Land)

Hans married **Margaretha Elisabeth Westphal**.[1] Margaretha was born in 1765.[267]

Children from this marriage were:

i.   **Anna Catarina Dorotea Ahrend**[268] was born in 1793.[268]

9   ii.   **Anna Catherina Hedewig Ahrend**[1] (born in 1797 in Klenau, Grube, Ostholstein, Holstein - died on 26 Jan 1846 in Neustadt, Ostholstein, Holstein). Anna married **Claus Friederich Weidemann**,[1] son of **Claus Hinrich Weidemann**[1] and **Anna Elsabe Dorothea Haack**,[1] on 21 Mar 1824 in Neustadt, Ostholstein, Holstein.[266] Claus was born on 10 Dec 1801 in Stolpe, Ostholstein, Holstein[265] and died on 9 Mar 1881 in Neustadt, Ostholstein, Holstein.[1]

19. Margaretha Elisabeth Westphal[1] was born in 1765.[267]

Noted events in her life were:
- Resided: 1803, Klenau, Grube, Ostholstein, Holstein.[268]

Margaretha married **Hans Jürgen Ahrend**.[1] Hans was born in 1766.[268] Another name for Hans was Juergen Arndt.[1]

Margaretha next married **Ausborn**.[268]

The child from this marriage was:

    i.   **Anna Sophia Margaretha Ausborn** was born in 1791.[268]

20. Carl Friedrich Wolf[120] was born in 1781,[269] died on 13 Apr 1835 in Schossow, Altenhagen, Pommern, Preußen,[269] and was buried on 15 Apr 1835.[270] The cause of his death was pleurisy.

Noted events in his life were:
- Occupation: weaver, 1810, Wolde, Röckwitz, Mecklenburg-Schwerin.[271]
- Occupation: weaver, before 1835, Schossow, Altenhagen, Pommern, Preußen.[270]

Carl married **Christina Dorothea Elisabeth Teage**[121] on 9 Nov 1810 in Zwiedorf, Röckwitz, Mecklenburg-Schwerin.[271] Christina was born on 7 Jun 1789 in Wolde, Röckwitz, Mecklenburg-Schwerin,[272] was christened on 10 Jun 1789 in Röckwitz, Mecklenburg-Schwerin,[273] died on 5 Nov 1861 in Wolkow, Wildberg, Pommern, Preußen,[274] and was buried on 17 Nov 1861.[274] Another name for Christina was Elisabeth Teege.

    Marriage Notes: Bride is a daughter of Johan Christian Taege, deceased Statthalter (foreman) in Wolde.[271]

Children from this marriage were:

    i.   **Carl Friederich Wolf**[120] was christened on 20 Oct 1811 in Röckwitz, Mecklenburg-Schwerin.[120]

    ii.   **Johanna Sophia Carolina Wolf**[120] was born on 31 Dec 1812 in Zwiedorf, Röckwitz, Mecklenburg-Schwerin[304] and was christened on 4 Jan 1813 in Röckwitz, Mecklenburg-Schwerin.[305]

10   iii.   **Johann Carl Friedrich Theodor "Carl" Wolf** (born on 7 Dec 1814 in Zwiedorf, Röckwitz, Mecklenburg-Schwerin - died on 20 Mar 1906 in Michigan City, LaPorte, Indiana). Johann married **Johanna Sophia Elisabeth "Elizabeth" Hillmann**, daughter of **Carl Friedrich Christian Hillmann** and **Christine Sophia Westphal**, about 1836.[132] Johanna was born on 31 May 1811 in Galenbeck, Stavenhagen, Mecklenburg-Schwerin,[133] was christened on 3 Jun 1811 in Kastorf, Stavenhagen, Mecklenburg-Schwerin,[134] and died on 16 Dec 1903 in Michigan City, LaPorte, Indiana.[135] Another name for Johanna was Elizabeth Hillman.[136]

    iv.   **Christina Sophia Wolf** was born on 21 Jun 1817 in Schossow, Altenhagen, Pommern, Preußen[306] and was christened on 27 Jun 1817 in Altenhagen, Pommern, Preußen.[306] Christina had a relationship with someone **Franz Christian Jacob Eick,** son of **Johann Friedrich Eick,** on 23 Mar 1844.[307] This couple did not marry.

    v.   **Caroline Elisabeth Wilhelmine Wolf** was born on 8 Sep 1819 in Schossow, Altenhagen, Pommern, Preußen,[308] was christened on 12 Sep 1819 in Altenhagen, Pommern, Preußen,[308] died on 27 Dec 1820 in Altenhagen, Pommern, Preußen[309] and was buried on 31 Dec 1820 in Altenhagen, Pommern, Preußen.[309]

    vi.   **Joachim Christian Friedrich Wolf** was born on 25 Jan 1822 in Schossow, Altenhagen, Pommern, Preußen,[310] was christened on 28 Jan 1822 in Altenhagen, Pommern, Preußen,[310] and died on 29 Sep 1891 in Röckwitz, Mecklenburg-Schwerin, Deutsches Reich.[311]

    vii.   **Christina Sophia Friederica Wolf** was born on 5 Jul 1824 in Schossow, Altenhagen, Pommern, Preußen[308] and was christened on 11 Jul 1824 in Altenhagen, Pommern, Preußen.[308]

viii.   **Johann Friedrich August Wolf** was born on 5 May 1833 in Schossow, Altenhagen, Pommern, Preußen,[312] was christened on 27 May 1833 in Altenhagen, Pommern, Preußen,[312] died on 28 Jul 1901 in Hermannshöhe, Pommern, Deutsches Reich,[313] and was buried on 31 Jul 1901 in Gültz, Pommern, Deutsches Reich.[313] The cause of his death was Altersschwäche (old age). Johann married **Maria Dorothea Luise Gielow,** daughter of **Joachim Friedrich Gielow**[314] and **Wilhelmina Elisabeth Böttcher,** on 3 Oct 1861 in Röckwitz, Mecklenburg-Schwerin.[314] Maria was born on 24 Dec 1834 in Röckwitz, Mecklenburg-Schwerin,[315] was christened on 4 Jan 1835 in Röckwitz, Mecklenburg-Schwerin,[316] and died on 30 Jan 1907 in Hermannshöhe, Pommern, Deutsches Reich.[317]

21. Christina Dorothea Elisabeth Teage,[121] daughter of **Johann Christian Teage**[120] and **Maria Dorothea Brüggert,**[120] was born on 7 Jun 1789 in Wolde, Röckwitz, Mecklenburg-Schwerin,[272] was christened on 10 Jun 1789 in Röckwitz, Mecklenburg-Schwerin,[273] died on 5 Nov 1861 in Wolkow, Wildberg, Pommern, Preußen,[274] and was buried on 17 Nov 1861.[274] Another name for Christina was Elisabeth Teege.

> Christening Notes: Sponsors were Anna Dorothea Daehn, daylaborer and Helmuth Pestlin's wife; Catharina Dorothea Schlicken, coachman and Taege's wife; and Jochen Christopher Laborn.

> Death Notes: She left behind 6 adult children.

Noted events in her life were:
• Resided: 1810, Wolde, Röckwitz, Mecklenburg-Schwerin.[271]

Christina married **Carl Friedrich Wolf**[120] on 9 Nov 1810 in Zwiedorf, Röckwitz, Mecklenburg-Schwerin.[271] Carl was born in 1781,[269] died on 13 Apr 1835 in Schossow, Altenhagen, Pommern, Preußen,[269] and was buried on 15 Apr 1835.[270] The cause of his death was pleurisy.

22. Carl Friedrich Christian Hillmann, son of **Jacob Hillmann,** was christened on 2 Jan 1768 in Galenbeck, Stavenhagen, Mecklenburg-Schwerin,[280] died on 9 Sep 1829 in Kastorf, Stavenhagen, Mecklenburg-Schwerin, and was buried on 11 Sep 1829.[281]

> Christening Notes: Sponsors were Herr von der Lancke, Leutnant von Schurtz, Frl. von Schurtz.

Noted events in his life were:
• Occupation: farmhand, 1799, Galenbeck, Stavenhagen, Mecklenburg-Schwerin.[282]
• Occupation: day laborer, 1819.[136]

Carl married **Christine Sophia Westphal** on 31 Oct 1799 in Galenbeck, Stavenhagen, Mecklenburg-Schwerin.[282] Christine was born about 1781 in Schwandt, Penzlin, Mecklenburg-Schwerin.[136]

Children from this marriage were:

i.   **Johann Friedrich Hillmann** was born on 1 Jun 1799 in Galenbeck, Stavenhagen, Mecklenburg-Schwerin[282] and was christened on 3 Jun 1799 in Kastorf, Stavenhagen, Mecklenburg-Schwerin.[282]

ii. **Johann Christian Hillmann**[318] was born on 12 Mar 1802 in Galenbeck, Stavenhagen, Mecklenburg-Schwerin,[318] was christened on 14 Mar 1802 in Kastorf, Stavenhagen, Mecklenburg-Schwerin,[318] and died on 23 Mar 1802.[318]

iii. **Henriette Caroline Sophie Hillmann**[319] was born on 12 Jul 1804 in Galenbeck, Stavenhagen, Mecklenburg-Schwerin,[320] was christened on 15 Jul 1804 in Kastorf, Stavenhagen, Mecklenburg-Schwerin,[319] and died on 22 Nov 1877 in Kastorf, Stavenhagen, Mecklenburg-Schwerin.

iv. **Maria Friederica Sophia Hillmann** [321] was born on 10 Aug 1806 in Galenbeck, Stavenhagen, Mecklenburg-Schwerin[322] and was christened on 10 Aug 1806 in Kastorf, Stavenhagen, Mecklenburg-Schwerin.[321]

v. **Catharina Dorothea Johanna Hillmann** [323] was born on 10 Nov 1808 in Galenbeck, Stavenhagen, Mecklenburg-Schwerin,[324] was christened on 13 Nov 1808 in Kastorf, Stavenhagen, Mecklenburg-Schwerin,[325] and died in Indiana.[56] Catharina married **Christian Friederich Theodor Paschen** on 12 Nov 1854 in Kastorf, Stavenhagen, Mecklenburg-Schwerin.[326] Christian was born on 28 Sep 1805 in Mecklenburg-Schwerin[181] and died on 9 Oct 1890 in Porter, Indiana.[56]

11 vi. **Johanna Sophia Elisabeth "Elizabeth" Hillmann** (born on 31 May 1811 in Galenbeck, Stavenhagen, Mecklenburg-Schwerin - died on 16 Dec 1903 in Michigan City, LaPorte, Indiana). Johanna married **Christian Martin Conrad,** son of **Frederick Conrad,** on 7 Sep 1832 in Galenbeck, Stavenhagen, Mecklenburg-Schwerin.[297] Christian was born in 1784 in Rosenow, Stavenhagen, Pommern, Preußen[136] and died after 1833 in Galenbeck, Stavenhagen, Mecklenburg-Schwerin. Johanna next married **Johann Carl Friedrich Theodor "Carl" Wolf,** son of **Carl Friedrich Wolf**[120] and **Christina Dorothea Elisabeth Teage,**[121] about 1836.[132] Johann was born on 7 Dec 1814 in Zwiedorf, Röckwitz, Mecklenburg-Schwerin,[122] was christened on 11 Dec 1814 in Röckwitz, Mecklenburg-Schwerin,[123] died on 20 Mar 1906 in Michigan City, LaPorte, Indiana,[124] and was buried in Greenwood Cemetery, Michigan City, LaPorte, Indiana.[56] Other names for Johann were Carl Wolff, Charles Wolff, and Karl Wolff.

vii. **Johann Friedrich Gustav Hillmann** was born on 2 Oct 1813 in Galenbeck, Stavenhagen, Mecklenburg-Schwerin[327] and was christened on 10 Oct 1813 in Kastorf, Stavenhagen, Mecklenburg-Schwerin.[328]

viii. **Johann Christian Friedrich Hillmann** was born on 17 Mar 1816 in Galenbeck, Stavenhagen, Mecklenburg-Schwerin,[329] was christened on 24 Mar 1816 in Kastorf, Stavenhagen, Mecklenburg-Schwerin,[330] and died on 20 May 1817.

ix. **Carolina Sophia Friederica Hillmann** was born on 29 Sep 1818 in Galenbeck, Stavenhagen, Mecklenburg-Schwerin[331] and was christened on 4 Oct 1818 in Kastorf, Stavenhagen, Mecklenburg-Schwerin.[332]

23. Christine Sophia Westphal, daughter of **Johann Westphal,** was born about 1781 in Schwandt, Penzlin, Mecklenburg-Schwerin.[136]

Christine married **Carl Friedrich Christian Hillmann** on 31 Oct 1799 in Galenbeck, Stavenhagen, Mecklenburg-Schwerin.[282] Carl was christened on 2 Jan 1768 in Galenbeck, Stavenhagen, Mecklenburg-Schwerin,[280] died on 9 Sep 1829 in Kastorf, Stavenhagen, Mecklenburg-Schwerin, and was buried on 11 Sep 1829.[281]

Ancestor Report

Sixth Generation (3rd Great-Grandparents)

32. Hans Hinrich Weidemann,[1] son of **Hans Hinrich Weidemann**[1] and **Maria Elisabeth Schumacher**,[1] was christened on 7 Jan 1748 in Stolpe, Ostholstein, Holstein[1] and died on 13 Jan 1812 in Stolpe, Ostholstein, Holstein.[1]

General Notes: He worked a farm as a serf in Stolpe and when he was freed he became a landowner in 1793.

Noted events in his life were:
- Occupation: farmer (Hufner), Stolpe, Ostholstein, Holstein.[1]
- Occupation: day-laborer and farmhand with land (Tagelöhner und Inste mit Land), 1803, Stolpe, Ostholstein, Holstein.[301]

Hans married **Anna Margaretha Schumacher**[1] on 12 Oct 1776 in Altenkrempe, Ostholstein, Holstein.[1] Anna was christened on 19 Jul 1746 in Kassau, Ostholstein, Holstein[1] and died on 16 Dec 1818 in Kassau, Ostholstein, Holstein.[1] Another name for Anna was Greta.[301]

Children from this marriage were:

  i. **Ida Friederica Elisabeth Weidemann**[1] was born on 7 Mar 1778 in Stolpe, Ostholstein, Holstein[1] and died on 19 Jun 1785 in Stolpe, Ostholstein, Holstein.[1]

16 ii. **Claus Hinrich Weidemann**[1] (born on 8 May 1780 in Stolpe, Ostholstein, Holstein - died on 1 Dec 1857 in Kassau, Ostholstein, Holstein). Claus married **Anna Elsabe Dorothea Haack**,[1] daughter of **Hans Detlef Haack**[1] and **Anna Elsabe Diekmann**,[1] on 11 Oct 1800 in Altenkrempe, Ostholstein, Holstein.[1] Anna was born on 30 Jun 1777 in Kassau, Ostholstein, Holstein[1] and died on 2 Feb 1855 in Kassau, Ostholstein, Holstein.[1]

  iii. **Ida Catharina Margaretha Weidemann**[1] was born on 7 May 1783 in Stolpe, Ostholstein, Holstein.[1] Ida married **Johann Friedrich Schlichting**,[1] son of **Hans Hinrich Schlichting**[1] and **Anna Margaretha**,[1] on 21 Jun 1811 in Altenkrempe, Ostholstein, Holstein.[1]

  iv. **Ida Christina Henrietta Weidemann**[1] was born on 9 Jul 1790 in Stolpe, Ostholstein, Holstein.[1] Another name for Ida was Ida Christina Henrietta Prüß. Ida married **Jürgen Hinrich Prüß**,[1] son of **Claus Prüß** and **Dorothea Bock**,[1] on 28 Oct 1790 in Altenkrempe, Ostholstein, Holstein.[1]

33. Anna Margaretha Schumacher,[1] daughter of **Hinrich Schumacher**[1] and **Hedwig Wehde**,[1] was christened on 19 Jul 1746 in Kassau, Ostholstein, Holstein[1] and died on 16 Dec 1818 in Kassau, Ostholstein, Holstein.[1] Another name for Anna was Greta.[301]

Anna married **Hans Hinrich Weidemann**[1] on 12 Oct 1776 in Altenkrempe, Ostholstein, Holstein.[1] Hans was christened on 7 Jan 1748 in Stolpe, Ostholstein, Holstein[1] and died on 13 Jan 1812 in Stolpe, Ostholstein, Holstein.[1]

34. Hans Detlef Haack.[1]

Noted events in his life were:
- Occupation: laborer, Kassau, Ostholstein, Holstein.[1]

Hans married **Anna Elsabe Diekmann**[1] circa 1775.[1]

The child from this marriage was:

17   i.   **Anna Elsabe Dorothea Haack**[1] (born on 30 Jun 1777 in Kassau, Ostholstein, Holstein - died on 2 Feb 1855 in Kassau, Ostholstein, Holstein). Anna married **Claus Hinrich Weidemann**,[1] son of **Hans Hinrich Weidemann**[1] and **Anna Margaretha Schumacher**,[1] on 11 Oct 1800 in Altenkrempe, Ostholstein, Holstein.[1] Claus was born on 8 May 1780 in Stolpe, Ostholstein, Holstein[1] and died on 1 Dec 1857 in Kassau, Ostholstein, Holstein.[1]

35. Anna Elsabe Diekmann.[1]

Anna married **Hans Detlef Haack**[1] circa 1775.[1]

42. Johann Christian Teage,[120] son of **Johann Tege**, died on 19 Jan 1810 in Wolde, Röckwitz, Mecklenburg-Schwerin[271] and was buried on 21 Jan 1810.[271]

> Research Notes: His father may have been "the old Johann Tege from Marko" who was buried on 25 Aug 1776. His children were Johann Christian, Christian Friedrich, and Johann Caspar. [333]

Noted events in his life were:
- Occupation: foreman, 1782, Kastorf, Stavenhagen, Mecklenburg-Schwerin.[275]

- Occupation: Statthalter (foreman), 1810, Wolde, Röckwitz, Mecklenburg-Schwerin.[271]

Johann married **Eleonora Schmidt**[334] on 3 Jan 1777 in Kastorf, Stavenhagen, Mecklenburg-Schwerin.[334] Eleonora died on 1 Mar 1782 in Kastorf, Stavenhagen, Mecklenburg-Schwerin.[275]

The child from this marriage was:

i.   **Johann Friedrich Teage** was born on 12 Jan 1780 in Kastorf, Stavenhagen, Mecklenburg-Schwerin[335] and was christened on 16 Jan 1780 in Kastorf, Stavenhagen, Mecklenburg-Schwerin.[335]

Johann next married **Maria Dorothea Brüggert**[120] on 17 May 1782 in Kastorf, Stavenhagen, Mecklenburg-Schwerin.[275] Maria was born on 20 Oct 1757 in Kastorf, Stavenhagen, Mecklenburg-Schwerin,[276] died on 4 Feb 1821 in Kastorf, Stavenhagen, Mecklenburg-Schwerin,[277] and was buried on 7 Feb 1821.[277]

Children from this marriage were:

i.   **Hanna Catharina Maria Teage** was born on 22 Feb 1784 in Kastorf, Stavenhagen, Mecklenburg-Schwerin[336] and was christened on 24 Feb 1784 in Kastorf, Stavenhagen, Mecklenburg-Schwerin.[336]

ii.   **Carl Friedrich Teage** was born on 28 Jun 1787 in Kastorf, Stavenhagen, Mecklenburg-Schwerin[337] and was christened on 30 Jun 1787 in Kastorf, Stavenhagen, Mecklenburg-Schwerin.[337] Carl married **Sophia Dorothea Drews**, daughter of **Joachim Drews**, on 27 Oct 1809 in Röckwitz, Mecklenburg-Schwerin.[338]

21   iii.   **Christina Dorothea Elisabeth Teage**[121] (born on 7 Jun 1789 in Wolde, Röckwitz, Mecklenburg-Schwerin - died on 5 Nov 1861 in Wolkow, Wildberg, Pommern, Preußen). Christina married **Carl Friedrich Wolf**[120] on 9 Nov 1810 in Zwiedorf, Röckwitz, Mecklenburg-Schwerin.[271] Carl was born in 1781,[269] died on 13 Apr 1835 in Schossow, Altenhagen, Pommern, Preußen,[269] and was buried on 15 Apr 1835.[270] The cause of his death was pleurisy.

iv.   **Johann Friedrich Theodor Teage** was born on 2 Apr 1793 in Wolde, Röckwitz,

Mecklenburg-Schwerin[339] and was christened on 5 Apr 1793 in Röckwitz, Mecklenburg-Schwerin.[340]

43. Maria Dorothea Brüggert,[120] daughter of **Thomas Christian Brüggert** and **Catharina Dorothea Ebert,** was born on 20 Oct 1757 in Kastorf, Stavenhagen, Mecklenburg-Schwerin,[276] died on 4 Feb 1821 in Kastorf, Stavenhagen, Mecklenburg-Schwerin,[277] and was buried on 7 Feb 1821.[277]

> Christening Notes: The sponsors were Sophia Dorothea Lüthen, Maria Virgils, and Friedrich Maß.

Maria married **Johann Christian Teage**[120] on 17 May 1782 in Kastorf, Stavenhagen, Mecklenburg-Schwerin.[275] Johann died on 19 Jan 1810 in Wolde, Röckwitz, Mecklenburg-Schwerin[271] and was buried on 21 Jan 1810.[271]

44. Jacob Hillmann,[283] son of **Hillmann**.

Jacob married someone.

His children were:

	i.	**Maria Dorothea Hillmann** was christened on 29 Aug 1764 in Galenbeck, Stavenhagen, Mecklenburg-Schwerin.[341]
	ii.	**Florentina Sophia Hillmann** was christened on 28 Feb 1767 in Rosenow, Stavenhagen, Pommern, Preußen.[342]
22	iii.	**Carl Friedrich Christian Hillmann** (christened on 2 Jan 1768 in Galenbeck, Stavenhagen, Mecklenburg-Schwerin - died on 9 Sep 1829 in Kastorf, Stavenhagen, Mecklenburg-Schwerin). Carl married **Christine Sophia Westphal,** daughter of **Johann Westphal,** on 31 Oct 1799 in Galenbeck, Stavenhagen, Mecklenburg-Schwerin.[282] Christine was born about 1781 in Schwandt, Penzlin, Mecklenburg-Schwerin.[136]
	iv.	**Johann Heinrich Hillmann** was christened on 11 Feb 1770 in Galenbeck, Stavenhagen, Mecklenburg-Schwerin.[343] Johann married **Henriette Krüger**.
	v.	**Jochen Erdmann Hillmann**[344] was born on 10 Aug 1775 in Galenbeck, Stavenhagen, Mecklenburg-Schwerin[344] and was christened on 13 Aug 1775 in Kastorf, Stavenhagen, Mecklenburg-Schwerin.[344]

46. Johann Westphal.

> Noted events in his life were:
> • Occupation: farmhand, 1799, Galenbeck, Stavenhagen, Mecklenburg-Schwerin.[282]

Johann married someone.

His child was:

23	i.	**Christine Sophia Westphal** (born about 1781 in Schwandt, Penzlin, Mecklenburg-Schwerin). Christine married **Carl Friedrich Christian Hillmann,** son of **Jacob Hillmann,** on 31 Oct 1799 in Galenbeck, Stavenhagen, Mecklenburg-Schwerin.[282] Carl was christened on 2 Jan 1768 in Galenbeck, Stavenhagen, Mecklenburg-Schwerin,[280] died on 9 Sep 1829 in Kastorf, Stavenhagen, Mecklenburg-Schwerin, and was buried on 11 Sep 1829.[281]

Ancestor Report

Seventh Generation (4th Great-Grandparents)

64. Hans Hinrich Weidemann,[1] son of **Hans Hinrich Weidemann**[1] and **Engel Muuß**,[284] was born about 1714 in Kassau, Ostholstein, Holstein[1] and died on 11 Jan 1798 in Stolpe, Ostholstein, Holstein.[1]

> General Notes: He was a serf for the Danish Count von Brockdorff, who took over the estate from the von Dernath's in 1730.

Noted events in his life were:
- Occupation: farmer of large farm (Hufner), Stolpe, Ostholstein, Holstein.[1]

Hans married **Maria Elisabeth Schumacher**[1] on 6 Nov 1746 in Altenkrempe, Ostholstein, Holstein.[1] Maria was born about 1715 in Sierhagen, Ostholstein, Holstein[1] and died on 25 Apr 1792 in Stolpe, Ostholstein, Holstein.[1]

Children from this marriage were:

    i.   **Magdalena Dorothea Weidemann**[1] was christened on 25 May 1742 in Stolpe, Ostholstein, Holstein[1] and died on 5 Apr 1794 in Stolpe, Ostholstein, Holstein.[1]

32   ii.   **Hans Hinrich Weidemann**[1] (christened on 7 Jan 1748 in Stolpe, Ostholstein, Holstein - died on 13 Jan 1812 in Stolpe, Ostholstein, Holstein). Hans married **Anna Margaretha Schumacher**,[1] daughter of **Hinrich Schumacher**[1] and **Hedwig Wehde**,[1] on 12 Oct 1776 in Altenkrempe, Ostholstein, Holstein.[1] Anna was christened on 19 Jul 1746 in Kassau, Ostholstein, Holstein[1] and died on 16 Dec 1818 in Kassau, Ostholstein, Holstein.[1] Another name for Anna was Greta.[301]

    iii.   **Claus Friedrich Weidemann**[1] was christened on 27 Nov 1751 in Stolpe, Ostholstein, Holstein[1] and died on 14 Nov 1819 in Stolpe, Ostholstein, Holstein.[1] Claus married **Ida Margaretha Nuessen**[1] on 12 Oct 1798 in Altenkrempe, Ostholstein, Holstein. Ida was christened on 30 Oct 1768 in Stolpe, Ostholstein, Holstein.[345] Another name for Ida was Ida Nøssen.

    iv.   **Anna Margaretha Elisabeth Weidemann**[1] was christened on 22 Jan 1758 in Stolpe, Ostholstein, Holstein[1] and died on 9 Aug 1772 in Stolpe, Ostholstein, Holstein.[1] The cause of her death was diarrhea.

65. Maria Elisabeth Schumacher,[1] daughter of **Jochen Schumacher**[1] and **Sophia**,[1] was born about 1715 in Sierhagen, Ostholstein, Holstein[1] and died on 25 Apr 1792 in Stolpe, Ostholstein, Holstein.[1]

Maria married **Hans Hinrich Weidemann**[1] on 6 Nov 1746 in Altenkrempe, Ostholstein, Holstein.[1] Hans was born about 1714 in Kassau, Ostholstein, Holstein[1] and died on 11 Jan 1798 in Stolpe, Ostholstein, Holstein.[1]

66. Hinrich Schumacher.[1]

Noted events in his life were:
- Occupation: cow-heardsman (Kuhhirte) at Sierhagen estate, Sierhagen, Ostholstein, Holstein.[1]
- Residence: Kassau, Ostholstein, Holstein.[1]

Hinrich married **Hedwig Wehde**.[1] Another name for Hedwig was Heilwich Wehde.[1]

The child from this marriage was:

33   i.   **Anna Margaretha Schumacher**[1] (christened on 19 Jul 1746 in Kassau, Ostholstein, Holstein - died on 16 Dec 1818 in Kassau, Ostholstein, Holstein). Anna

married **Hans Hinrich Weidemann**,[1] son of **Hans Hinrich Weidemann**[1] and **Maria Elisabeth Schumacher**,[1] on 12 Oct 1776 in Altenkrempe, Ostholstein, Holstein.[1] Hans was christened on 7 Jan 1748 in Stolpe, Ostholstein, Holstein[1] and died on 13 Jan 1812 in Stolpe, Ostholstein, Holstein.[1]

67. Hedwig Wehde.[1] Another name for Hedwig was Heilwich Wehde.[1]

Hedwig married **Hinrich Schumacher**.[1]

84. Johann Tege died on 25 Aug 1776 in Borgfeld, Stavenhagen, Mecklenburg-Schwerin.[278]

> Research Notes: Johann Tege is likely Johann Christian Taege's father, but it has not been proven.

Noted events in his life were:
- Resided: Markow, Borgfeld AG Stavenhagen, Mecklenburg-Schwerin.[278]

Johann married someone.

His children were:

42   i.   **Johann Christian Teage**[120] (died on 19 Jan 1810 in Wolde, Röckwitz, Mecklenburg-Schwerin). Johann married **Eleonora Schmidt**[334] on 3 Jan 1777 in Kastorf, Stavenhagen, Mecklenburg-Schwerin.[334] Eleonora died on 1 Mar 1782 in Kastorf, Stavenhagen, Mecklenburg-Schwerin.[275] Johann next married **Maria Dorothea Brüggert**,[120] daughter of **Thomas Christian Brüggert** and **Catharina Dorothea Ebert,** on 17 May 1782 in Kastorf, Stavenhagen, Mecklenburg-Schwerin.[275] Maria was born on 20 Oct 1757 in Kastorf, Stavenhagen, Mecklenburg-Schwerin,[276] died on 4 Feb 1821 in Kastorf, Stavenhagen, Mecklenburg-Schwerin,[277] and was buried on 7 Feb 1821.[277]

     ii.   **Christian Friedrich Teage**. Christian married **Christina Rebecca Henning**.

     iii.   **Johann Caspar Teage**. Johann married **Catharina Elisabeth Schlicker** on 9 Nov 1784.[347]

86. Thomas Christian Brüggert.

Thomas married **Catharina Dorothea Ebert** on 20 Oct 1755 in Kastorf, Stavenhagen, Mecklenburg-Schwerin.[279]

The child from this marriage was:

43   i.   **Maria Dorothea Brüggert**[120] (born on 20 Oct 1757 in Kastorf, Stavenhagen, Mecklenburg-Schwerin - died on 4 Feb 1821 in Kastorf, Stavenhagen, Mecklenburg-Schwerin). Maria married **Johann Christian Teage**,[120] son of **Johann Tege,** on 17 May 1782 in Kastorf, Stavenhagen, Mecklenburg-Schwerin.[275] Johann died on 19 Jan 1810 in Wolde, Röckwitz, Mecklenburg-Schwerin[271] and was buried on 21 Jan 1810.[271]

87. Catharina Dorothea Ebert.

Catharina married **Thomas Christian Brüggert** on 20 Oct 1755 in Kastorf, Stavenhagen, Mecklenburg-Schwerin.[279]

88. Hillmann.

Hillmann married someone.

His children were:

44   i.   **Jacob Hillmann**.[283] Jacob married someone.

    ii.   **Johann Friedrich Hillmann** died on 14 Jan 1821 in Kastorf, Stavenhagen, Mecklenburg-Schwerin[283] and was buried on 16 Jan 1821.[283] Another name for Johann was Helmann.

    iii.   **Ana Dorothea Hillmann**[283]

Ancestor Report

Eighth Generation (5th Great-Grandparents)

128. Hans Hinrich Weidemann[1] was born circa 1680.[1]

> General Notes: Hans was a serf in Kassau, which lies on the Sierhagen estate. The old manor house, Gut Sierhagen, is about a half mile south of Kassau. The lord of the manor during Hans's life was the Count von Dernath.

> Noted events in his life were:
> • Occupation: serf-farmer with a large farm (Hufner), Kassau, Ostholstein, Holstein.[1]

Hans married **Engel Muuß**[284] before 1714 in Gemeinde Altenkrempe, Ostholstein, Holstein.[1] Engel was christened on 25 Jul 1680 in Süsel, Ostholstein, Holstein.[285]

Children from this marriage were:

> 64   i.   **Hans Hinrich Weidemann**[1] (born about 1714 in Kassau, Ostholstein, Holstein - died on 11 Jan 1798 in Stolpe, Ostholstein, Holstein). Hans married **Maria Elisabeth Schumacher**,[1] daughter of **Jochen Schumacher**[1] and **Sophia**,[1] on 6 Nov 1746 in Altenkrempe, Ostholstein, Holstein.[1] Maria was born about 1715 in Sierhagen, Ostholstein, Holstein[1] and died on 25 Apr 1792 in Stolpe, Ostholstein, Holstein.[1]

>   ii.   **August Friedrich "Gust" Weidemann**[1] was born about 1719 in Kassau, Ostholstein, Holstein[1] and died on 10 Jun 1787 in Kassau, Ostholstein, Holstein.[1]

129. Engel Muuß,[284] daughter of **Hans Muuß**[286] and **Margreth Bück**,[287] was christened on 25 Jul 1680 in Süsel, Ostholstein, Holstein.[285]

> Research Notes: Probably resided in the villiage of Roge on the estate of Oevelgönne.

Engel married **Hans Hinrich Weidemann**[1] before 1714 in Gemeinde Altenkrempe, Ostholstein, Holstein.[1] Hans was born circa 1680.[1]

130. Jochen Schumacher[1] was born Est 1680.[1]

> Noted events in his life were:
> • Occupation: small farmer (Kätner), Sierhagen, Ostholstein, Holstein.[1]

Jochen married **Sophia**.[1] Sophia was born Est 1680.[1]

The child from this marriage was:

> 65   i.   **Maria Elisabeth Schumacher**[1] (born about 1715 in Sierhagen, Ostholstein, Holstein - died on 25 Apr 1792 in Stolpe, Ostholstein, Holstein). Maria married **Hans Hinrich Weidemann**,[1] son of **Hans Hinrich Weidemann**[1] and **Engel Muuß**,[284] on 6 Nov 1746 in Altenkrempe, Ostholstein, Holstein.[1] Hans was born about 1714 in Kassau, Ostholstein, Holstein[1] and died on 11 Jan 1798 in Stolpe, Ostholstein, Holstein.[1]

131. Sophia[1] was born Est 1680.[1]

Sophia married **Jochen Schumacher**.[1] Jochen was born Est 1680.[1]

Ancestor Report

Ninth Generation (6th Great-Grandparents)

258. Hans Muuß[286] was born Est 1655.[287]

General Notes: A serf on the Övelgönne estate.

Research Notes: His father is thought to be Hans Muuss of Roge, Sierksdorf, a small village between Neustadt and Süsel within the lands of the Övelgönne estate, according to the research of genealogist Ilkka Westergren. They were married and their children were baptised in St. Laurentius Church in Süsel. [288]

Hans married **Margreth Bück**[287] on 25 Aug 1678 in Süsel, Ostholstein, Holstein.[287] Another name for Margreth was Grete.

Children from this marriage were:

      i.   **Hans Muuß**[286] was christened on 26 Jan 1679 in Süsel, Ostholstein, Holstein.[287]

129 ii.   **Engel Muuß**[284] (christened on 25 Jul 1680 in Süsel, Ostholstein, Holstein). Engel married **Hans Hinrich Weidemann**[1] before 1714 in Gemeinde Altenkrempe, Ostholstein, Holstein.[1] Hans was born circa 1680.[1]

    iii.   **Claus Muuß**[286] was christened on 24 Jun 1683 in Süsel, Ostholstein, Holstein.[286]

    iv.   **Hinrich Muuß**[286] was christened on 24 Jun 1683 in Süsel, Ostholstein, Holstein,[287] died on 5 Aug 1773 in Sirckesdorp, Ostholstein, Holstein,[286] and was buried on 8 Aug 1773 in Süsel, Ostholstein, Holstein.[286] Hinrich married **Anna Catharina Marckmann**[286] on 17 Apr 1718 in Süsel, Ostholstein, Holstein.[287] Anna was christened on 6 Nov 1698 in Strande, Ostholstein, Holstein[288] and died Est 1728.[348] Hinrich next married **Catharina Magdalena Steffen**[287] Est 1729.[287] Catharina was born Est 1707 in Strande, Ostholstein, Holstein[288] and died on 3 Feb 1763.[288]

    v.   **Trincke Muuß**[286] was christened on 9 Sep 1694 in Süsel, Ostholstein, Holstein.[287]

259. Margreth Bück.[287] Another name for Margreth was Grete.

Margreth married **Hans Muuß**[286] on 25 Aug 1678 in Süsel, Ostholstein, Holstein.[287] Hans was born Est 1655.[287]

Picture Album for Alma Marie Weidemann

Alma Marie Swanson née Weidemann (1904-2004)

Photo courtesy of R. Swanson/M. Haite.

Picture Album for Alma Marie Weidemann

Alma Weidemann

Photo courtesy of R. Swanson/M. Haite.
(about 1906)

Picture Album for Alma Marie Weidemann

Alma Weidemann

Photo courtesy of R. Swanson/M. Haite.

Picture Album for Alma Marie Weidemann

Alma Weidemann

Photo courtesy of R. Swanson/M. Haite.

Picture Album for Alma Marie Weidemann

Alma Weidemann

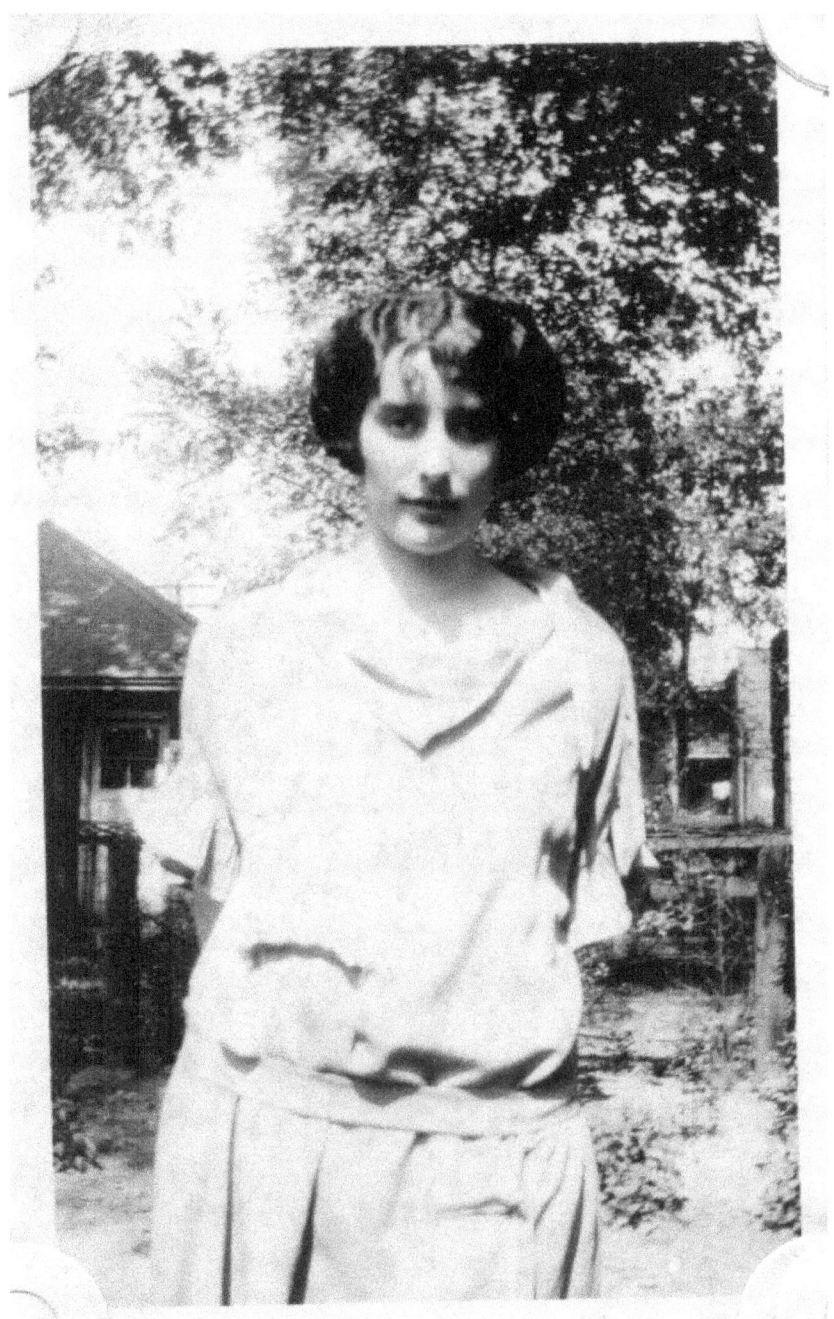

Photo courtesy of R. Swanson/M. Haite.

Picture Album for Alma Marie Weidemann

Alma Weidemann

Photo courtesy of R. Swanson/M. Haite.

Picture Album for Alma Marie Weidemann

Alma Weidemann

Photo courtesy of R. Swanson/M. Haite.

Picture Album for Alma Marie Weidemann

Alma Weidemann

Photo courtesy of R. Swanson/M. Haite.

Picture Album for Alma Marie Weidemann

Alma Weidemann

Photo courtesy of R. Swanson/M. Haite.

Picture Album for Alma Marie Weidemann

Alma Weidemann

Photo courtesy of R. Swanson/M. Haite.

Picture Album for Alma Marie Weidemann

Alma Swanson

Photo courtesy of R. Swanson/M. Haite.

Picture Album for Alma Marie Weidemann

Swanson home and office in Vassar

Located at 220 N. Main St., Vassar. The garage is on the left and the doctor's office is on the right.
Photo courtesy of R. Swanson.

Picture Album for Alma Marie Weidemann

Swanson family Thanksgiving

In Vassar, Michigan.
Photo courtesy of R. Swanson.
(1942)

Picture Album for Alma Marie Weidemann

Alma and Ewald Swanson

In their backyard in Vassar.
Photo courtesy of R. Swanson/M. Haite.
(1958)

Picture Album for Alma Marie Weidemann

Alma and Ewald Swanson

Photo courtesy of R. Swanson/M. Haite.

Picture Album for Alma Marie Weidemann

Alma Swanson

Photo courtesy of R. Swanson.

Picture Album for Weidemann

Christian Weidemann (1837-1913)

Photo courtesy of Mark Swanson.

Picture Album for Weidemann

Christian Weidemann (1837-1913)

Photo courtesy of Mark Swanson.
(circa 1910)

Picture Album for Weidemann

Alma Weidemann (1876-1928)

Alma was guardian to her neice Alma Marie Weidemann beginning in 1920 after her
parents were killed.
Photo courtesy of R. Swanson/M. Haite.
(1899)

Picture Album for Weidemann

Christian Weidemann and granddaughter Alma Marie Weidemann

Photo courtesy of R. Swanson/M. Haite.
(about 1912)

Picture Album for Weidemann

Christian Weidemann's children

From Left: Mathilda, Walter, Oscar, Caroline, Alma, Emma, Laura.
Photo courtesy of R. Swanson/M. Haite.
(about 1890)

Picture Album for Weidemann

Oscar and Laura Weidemann

Photo courtesy of Mark Swanson.
(about 1875)

Picture Album for Weidemann

Oscar Weidemann (1871-1920)

Photo courtesy of R. Swanson/M. Haite.

Picture Album for Weidemann

Christian Weidemann's citizenship certificate

UNITED STATES OF AMERICA.

CERTIFICATE OF CITIZENSHIP.

STATE OF MICHIGAN, } ss.
COUNTY OF WAYNE,

The Circuit Court for the County of Wayne.

Be it Remembered, That at a session of the Circuit Court for the County of Wayne (the same being a court of record, having common law jurisdiction and a seal and clerk), held at the Circuit Court Room, in the city of Detroit, county of Wayne, on the *26* day of *Sept* in the year one thousand nine hundred and *Six*   *Christian Weidemann* an alien, above the age of twenty-one years, a native of *Germany* exhibited a petition praying to be admitted a *Citizen of the United States of America*, pursuant to the several Acts of Congress heretofore passed on that subject, and it appearing to the said court that he has declared on his oath before the *Clerk of said Court*

on the *14* day of *July* A. D. *1874* that it was bona fide his intention to become a citizen of the United States, and to renounce forever all allegiance and fidelity to any foreign prince, potentate, state or sovereignty whatsoever; and particularly to *William I* *Emperor of Germany* the *Christian Weidemann* having also made proof by competent testimony of *John Neiper and Frank Noah* citizen of the United States that he has resided in the State of Michigan upwards of one year, last past, and within the United States of America upwards of five years immediately preceding his application; and it appearing to the satisfaction of the court, that during that time the said applicant had behaved as a man of good moral character, attached to the principles of the constitution of the United States, and well disposed to the good order and happiness of the same; and it further appearing to the satisfaction of the said Court from the affidavits of the said applicant and of his witnesses that the said applicant does not disbelieve in and is not opposed to all organized government, and is not a member of or affiliated with any organization entertaining and teaching such disbelief in or opposition to all organized government, and that he does not advocate or teach the duty, necessity or propriety of the unlawful assaulting or killing of any officer or officers, either of specific individuals or of officers generally, of the government of the United States, or of any other organized government, because of his or their official character, and that he has not violated any of the provisions of an Act of Congress entitled "An Act to Regulate the Immigration of Aliens into the United States," approved March 3, 1903; and he having declared on his solemn oath before the said Court, that he would support the constitution of the United States, and that he did absolutely and entirely renounce and abjure all allegiance and fidelity to every foreign prince, potentate, state or sovereignty whatsoever, and particularly to *William II* the *Emperor of Germany* of whom he was a subject. thereupon said court admitted the said *Christian Weidemann* to become a *Citizen of the United States* and ordered that all the proceedings aforesaid, and the affidavits of the said applicant and of his said witnesses reciting and affirming the truth of every material fact requisite for naturalization be entered of record by the clerk of said court, and the same have been entered of record accordingly.

In Witness Whereof, I have hereunto set my hand and affixed the seal of the Circuit Court for the County of Wayne at Detroit, this *26* day of *Sept* in the year of our Lord

Document courtesy of M. Haite.
(1906)

Picture Album for Weidemann

Christian Weidemann's home on Monroe Ave. in downtown Detroit

Photo courtesy of M. Haite.
(before 1905)

Picture Album for Weidemann

Looking down Monroe Avenue in Detroit.

The Weidemann's lived on Monroe before they built their home on Erskine in 1905. They
lived within a block of Cadillac Square, which is pictured above.
Postcard in public domain.
(1908)

Picture Album for Weidemann

Weidemann home at 269 Erskine Street in Detroit

Christian Weidemann built this house in 1905. Mathilde Weidemann was living here in 1930. It is now a fraternity alumni house. In 1921 Detroit underwent a major street renumbering project, and the number of this home changed from 93 Erskine to 269 Erskine.
Photo courtesy of M. Haite.

Picture Album for Weidemann

SS Russia

Oscare Weidemann traveled on the SS Russia for his trip to Germany.
Graphic courtesy Stuart Cameron, in public domain.

Picture Album for Weidemann

Oscar Weidemann at Royal Art School in Berlin

Photo courtesy of M. Haite.
(1894)

Picture Album for Weidemann

Christian Weidemann and crew

Christian Weidemann poses with his interior decoration crew, including his son Oscar, in
Pennsylvania.
Photo courtesy of M. Haite.
(about 1910)

Picture Album for Weidemann

Oscar and Henry Weidemann in Hamburg

Photo courtesy of Mark Swanson.
(abt 1866)

Picture Album for Weidemann

Jakob Weidemann (1824-1865)

Jakob remained in Germany when his brothers Christian and Henry went to America.
Jacob ran a successful cigar company on Kremper Street in Neustadt.
Photo Courtesy of Mark Swanson

Picture Album for Weidemann

Jakob Weidemann's cigar company

Jakob Weidemann's home and shop were on Kremper Street in Neustadt in Holstein. Jakob
Weidemann was immigrant Christian Weidemann's brother.
Photo courtesy M. Haite.

Picture Album for Weidemann

Henry Weidemann (1835-1895)

Christian Weidemann's brother, Henrich, who immigrated in 1866.
Photo courtesy of R. Swanson/M. Haite.

Picture Album for Weidemann

Old Map of Neustadt in Holstein

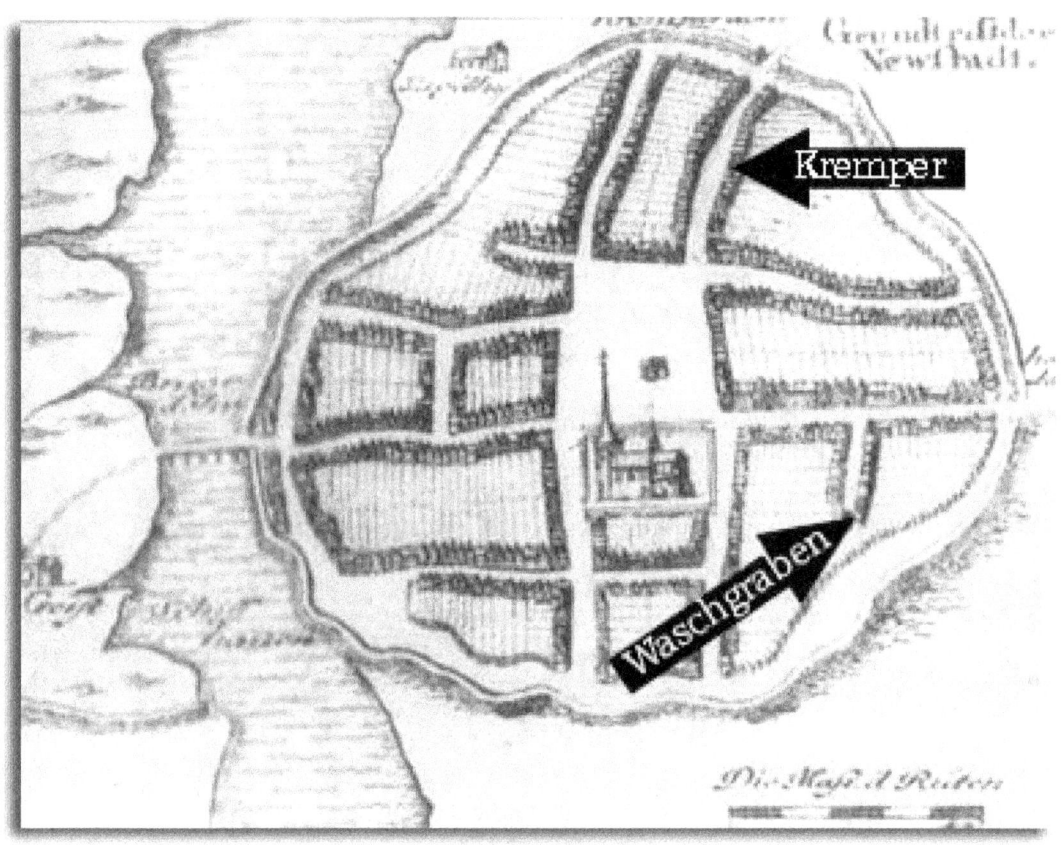

The Weidemann's lived on Waschgraben, and oldest son Jakob and father Claus later lived on Kremper Street.
Map in public domain.
(1649)

Picture Album for Weidemann

Kremper Street and the northern city gate

Photo in public domain
(about 1950)

Picture Album for Weidemann

75 pfennig note printed in Holstein

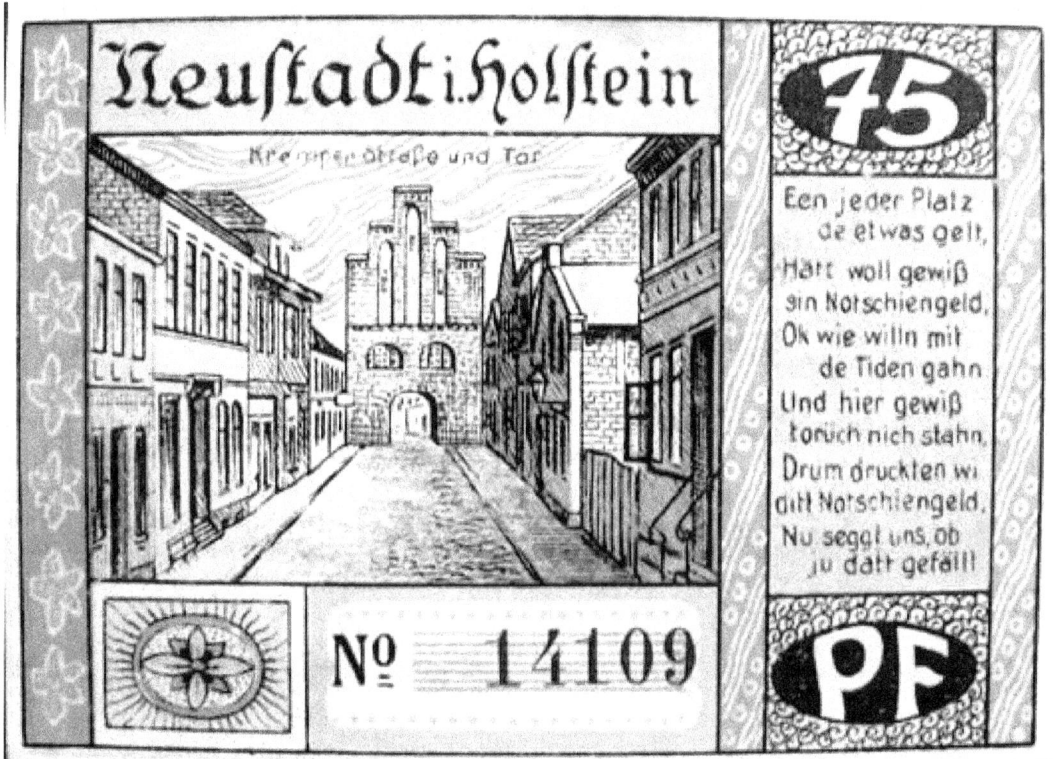

This German money shows Kremper Street and the northern city gate.
Photo in public domain
(1921)

Picture Album for Weidemann

Folk Festival in the square near Neustadt City Church

This brick gothic church on Neustadt's central marketplace square is the oldest building in
town. Christian Weidemann and his siblings were baptized here.
Photo in public domain.
(circa 1950)

Picture Album for Weidemann

Sketch by Oscar Weidemann of Neustadt House

The home where Christian Weidemann grew up on Waschgraben in Neustadt. The sketch shows the house number as 27.

(1894)

Picture Album for Weidemann

Christian Weidemann's home in Neustadt

This is probably the house where Christian Weidemann grew up. The home is on
Waschgraben in Neustadt.
Photo courtesy of Paul-Otto Irmert.
(2016)

Picture Album for Weidemann

The street called Waschgraben in Neustadt

Photo courtesy of Paul-Otto Irmert.
(2016)

Picture Album for Minahan/Moynahan

Mary E. Weidemann née Moynahan (1876-1920)

In Detroit. This is the only known picture of Mary Weidemann née Moynahan.
Photo courtesy of R. Swanson/M. Haite.
(about 1919)

Picture Album for Minahan/Moynahan

Croom, Limerick, Ireland

Old photo of High Street in Croom.
Photo in public domain / Croom National School.
(late 1800s)

Picture Album for Minahan/Moynahan

Croom, Limerick, Ireland

Old photo of High Street in Croom.
Photo in public domain / Croom National School.
(late 1800s)

Picture Album for Minahan/Moynahan

Croom, Limerick, Ireland

Recent photo of High Street in Croom.
Photo by Rebecca Swanson.
(2015)

St. Mary of the Assumption Church in Croom (Roman Catholic)

John Minahan and Mary O'Brien were married here in 1854.
Photo by Rebecca Swanson.
(2015)

Picture Album for Minahan/Moynahan

"New" Croom Castle

The new Croom castle between the River Maigue, St. Mary's Church, and in the
foreground the fair-green.
Photo by Rebecca Swanson.
(2015)

"Old" Croom Castle ruins

Part of the 12th century castle built by the O'Donovans in Croom.
Photo by Rebecca Swanson.
(2015)

Picture Album for Minahan/Moynahan

Death record for Mary Minahan née O'Brien

BUREAU OF VITAL STATISTICS
CITY OF ALBANY, NY

Gerald D. Jennings
Mayor

Denise C. Kelley
Registrar

FOR GENEALOGICAL PURPOSE ONLY

NAME OF DECEASED   Mary Monahan

DATE OF DEATH   6/18/1879   AGE   44   YEARS _____ MONTHS _____ DAYS

PLACE OF DEATH   44 Chestnut Street

RACE   White   SINGLE, MARRIED, WIDOWED   Married   NAME OF SPOUSE   not listed

PLACE OF BIRTH   Limerick, Ireland

OCCUPATION   not listed

FATHER   not listed   FATHER'S PLACE OF BIRTH   Ireland

MOTHER   not listed   MOTHER'S PLACE OF BIRTH   Ireland

CAUSE OF DEATH

CHIEF CAUSE   Carcinoma of Uterus

OTHER CAUSES

MEDICAL ATTENDANT   Dr. Franklin Townsen

PLACE OF BURIAL   St. Mary's Cemetery

NAME OF INFORMANT   Not listed

DATE RECORD FILED   7/9/1879   PAGE NUMBER   89   RECORD NUMBER   62

ADDITIONAL INFORMATION

STATE OF NEW YORK
CITY & COUNTY OF ALBANY
REGISTRAR OF VITAL STATISTICS

I, Denise C. Kelley, Registrar of Vital Statistics of the City of Albany, NY, DO HEREBY CERTIFY that the foregoing has been compared with the original record thereof on file in this office and do certify that the same is a correct transcript therefrom and of the whole thereof.

REGISTRAR

August 25, 2011
DATE

Extract from 1879 records.
Provided by the City of Albany.
(2014)

Picture Album for Minahan/Moynahan

Marriage certificate for Mary Moynahan and Oscar Weidemann

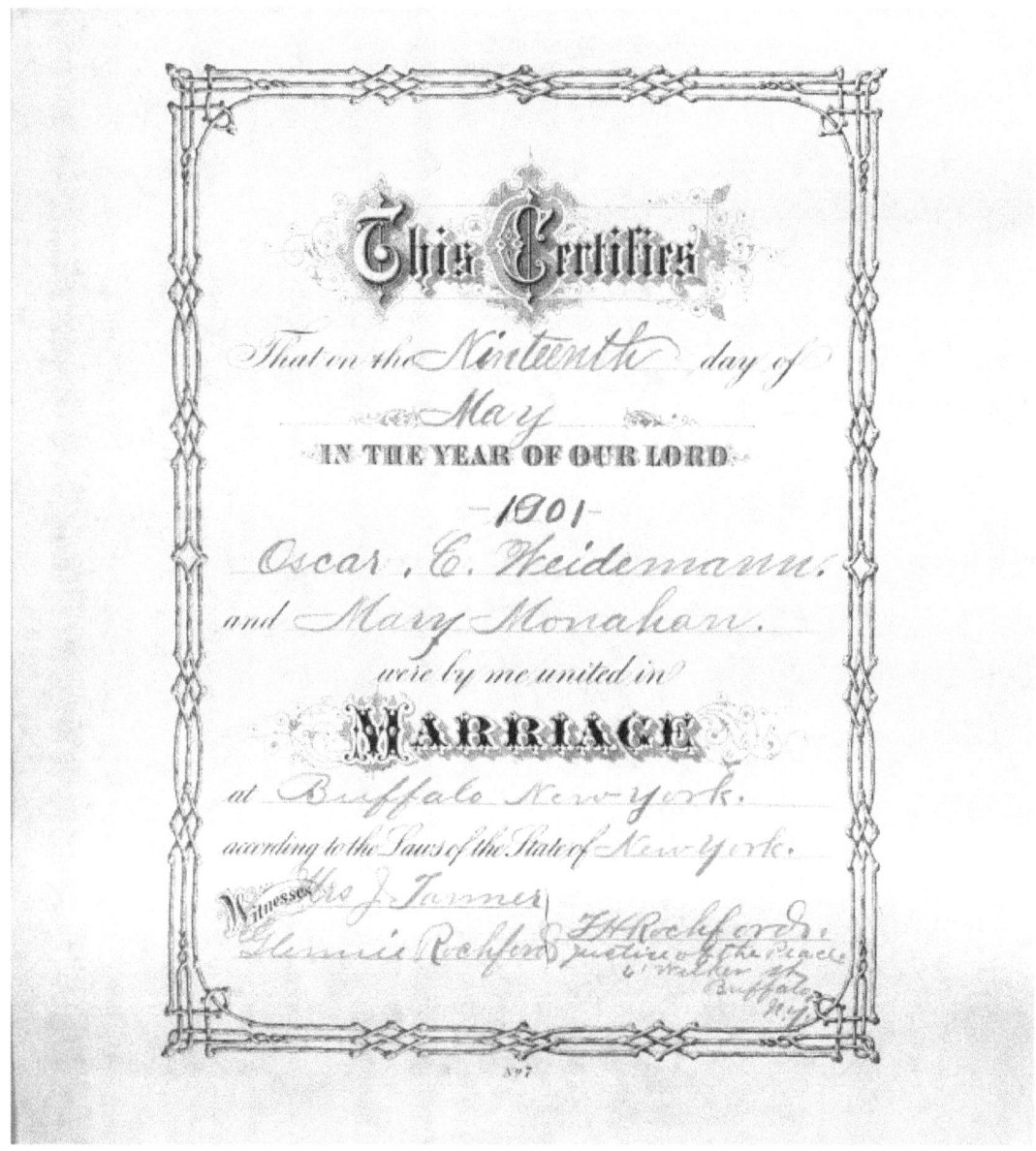

Signed in Buffalo, New York and sent to Oscar Weidemann in Erie, Pennsylvania.
Document courtesy of Richard Swanson.
(1901)

Picture Album for Minahan/Moynahan

Marriage certificate for Oscar Weidemann and Mary Moynahan

Provided by City of Buffalo, Erie, New York.
(1901)

Picture Album for Minahan/Moynahan

Naturalization application for John Minahan

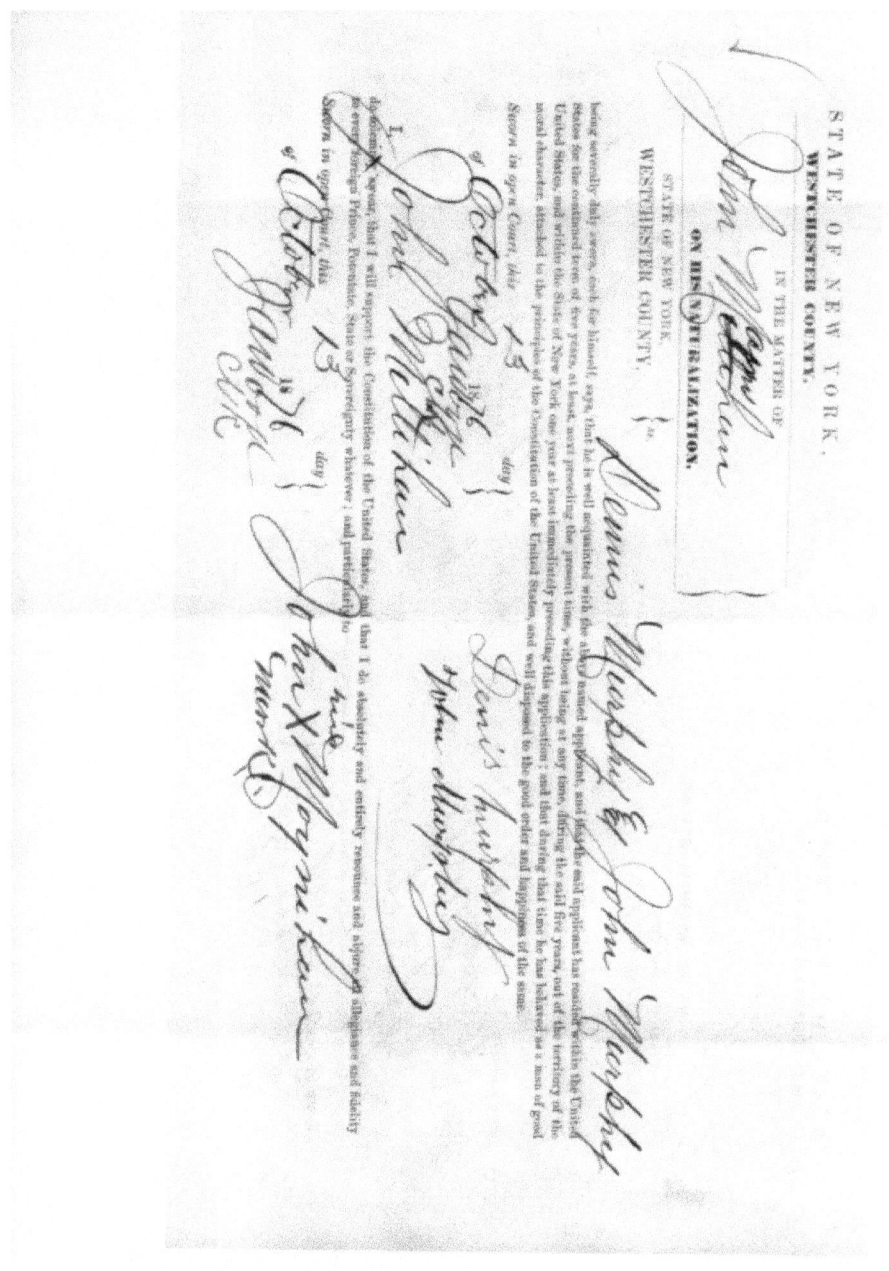

John Minahan's application for citizenship from Westchester County, New York is signed
with an X and his name is first spelled Millihan and then Moynihan.
Provided by the County of Westchester, New York.
(1876)

Picture Album for Wolf/Wolff

Mary Weidemann née Wolff (1841-1928)

Photo courtesy of M. Haite/R. Swanson.
(circa 1920)

Picture Album for Wolf/Wolff

Mary Weidemann née Wolff

Photo courtesy of M. Haite/R. Swanson.
(circa 1920)

Picture Album for Wolf/Wolff

Mary Weidemann née Wolff

Photo courtesy of M. Haite/R. Swanson.
(1923)

Picture Album for Wolf/Wolff

William Wallace Wolff and Lucille Perry in Miles City, Montana

Photo courtesy of Mark Swanson
(circa 1895)

Picture Album for Wolf/Wolff

Johann Carl Friedrich Theodor "Carl" Wolf (1814-1906)

Photo courtesy of M. Haite.
(circa 1900)

Picture Album for Wolf/Wolff

Kastorf Church (Lutheran)

Kastorf Church is a brick church built in 1788. Immigrant Carl Wolf married Elisabeth
Hillman here in 1811.
Photo in public domain.

Picture Album for Wolf/Wolff

Wildberg Church (Lutheran)

The Wildberg Church foundation was built in the 13th century, the altarpiece was made in 1612, and the square tower dates in the 18th century. Six of Carl Wolf and Elisabeth Hillmann's children were baptized in Wildberg Church.
Photo in public domain.

Picture Album for Wolf/Wolff

Wolkow Church (Lutheran)

The Wolkow Church dates from the 13th century and the altarpiece is from 1736. Mary
Wolf née Weidemann was baptized there in 1841.
Photo in public domain.

Picture Album for Wolf/Wolff

The Donau

The Wolf/Wolff family sailed to America on the Donau in 1858. The Donau was a 3-
masted, square-rigged sailing ship built in Altona, now part of Hamburg.
Print in public domain.
(1853)

Picture Album for Wolf/Wolff

Marriage certificate for Mary Wolff and Christian Weidemann

The were married in Detroit on 6 February 1868.
Document courtesy of M. Haite.
(1868)

Picture Album for Wolf/Wolff

Peter Elerbe

Peter Elerbe married Augusta Wolff in 1863 in Detroit.
Photo courtesy of Mark Swanson.
(circa 1870)

Source Citations

1. Wiebke Dannenberg, "The Weidemann Family from Stolpe, East-Holstein, Germany" (25 June 2005, unpublished document).

2. Ehles letter on Weidemann (24 April 1997 to Margery Haite). .... Wiebke Dannenberg, "The Weidemann Family from Stolpe, East-Holstein, Germany" (25 June 2005, unpublished document). .... Margery Haite, "Wolff Family" (5 typewritten pages, circa 1978). .... Michigan Death Records, 1897-1920 (seekingmichigan.com). .... Bob Strome, "Weidemann Family" (a five page type-written document). .... 1880 US Census. .... 1910 US Census. .... 1900 US Census. .... Death Certificate, Michigan Dept. of Community Health.

3. Ehles letter on Weidemann (24 April 1997 to Margery Haite). .... Margery Haite's handwritten notes to Richard Swanson. .... Margery Haite, "Wolff Family" (5 typewritten pages, circa 1978). .... Michigan Death Records, 1897-1920 (seekingmichigan.com). .... Bob Strome, "Weidemann Family" (a five page type-written document). .... Death Certificate, Michigan Dept. of Community Health.

4. Michigan Death Records, 1897-1920 (seekingmichigan.com).

5. Oscar Weidemann, Sketchbook (1894).

6. Henrich Weidemann, *Gedichte (Poetry)* (1897).

7. Hamburg Passenger Lists, 1850-1934 (ancestry.com). .... Henrich Weidemann, *Gedichte (Poetry)* (1897).

8. *Die Detroiter Abendpost,* 9 Nov 1895. .... Hamburg Passenger Lists, 1850-1934 (ancestry.com).

9. New York Passenger Lists, 1820-1957 (ancestry.com).

10. 1870 US Census.

11. Detroit City Directory For 1877 (umich.edu).

12. 1880 US Census.

13. Joint documents of the State of Michigan for the year 1889 Vol. 1.

14. 1900 US Census.

15. *Detroit Free Press,* April 16, 1905.

16. 1910 US Census.

17. Death Certificate, Michigan Dept. of Community Health.

18. *Detroit Free Press,* 23 Jun 1913.

19. Bob Strome, "Weidemann Family" (a five page type-written document). .... Michigan Marriages, 1851-1875 (ancestry.com).

20. Bob Strome, "Weidemann Family" (a five page type-written document). .... Hamburg Passenger Lists, 1850-1934 (ancestry.com). .... Margery Haite's handwritten notes to Richard Swanson. .... 1880 US Census. .... 1900 US Census. .... Wolkow Church Records.

21. Wolkow Church Records, 10/1841, p.15.

22. Bob Strome, "Weidemann Family" (a five page type-written document). .... Margery Haite's handwritten notes to Richard Swanson.

Source Citations

23. Hamburg Passenger Lists, 1850-1934 (ancestry.com).

24. 1920 US Census.

25. Stephen P. Morse Geneaology Resources (http://stevemorse.org/census/changes/DetroitDE.htm).

26. Bob Strome, "Weidemann Family" (a five page type-written document).

27. Bob Strome, "Weidemann Family" (a five page type-written document). .... Michigan, Births and Christenings Index, 1867-1911 (ancestry.com).

28. Bob Strome, "Weidemann Family" (a five page type-written document). .... 1880 US Census. .... 1870 US Census. .... 1900 US Census. .... 1920 US Census. .... 1930 US Census. .... 1910 US Census. .... Michigan, Death Certificates, 1921-1952 (familysearch.org).

29. Bob Strome, "Weidemann Family" (a five page type-written document). .... Michigan, Death Certificates, 1921-1952 (familysearch.org).

30. Bob Strome, "Weidemann Family" (a five page type-written document). .... Michigan Marriages, 1822-1995 (familysearch.org).

31. Bob Strome, "Weidemann Family" (a five page type-written document). .... U.S. Passport Applications, 1795-1925 (ancestry.com). .... 1880 US Census. .... 1910 US Census. .... 1920 US Census.

32. Marriage certificate and record for Mary Monahan and Christian Weidemann (Erie County, NY, 1901).

33. Bob Strome, "Weidemann Family" (a five page type-written document). .... 1880 US Census. .... 1900 US Census. .... 1910 US Census.

34. Bob Strome, "Weidemann Family" (a five page type-written document). .... *Detroit Free Press,* 17 Feb 1961.

35. *Journal of Proceedings Detroit Board of Education,* 1945.

36. Detroit Normal Training School graduation program (1895).

37. U.S. City Directories, 1821-1989 (ancestry.com).

38. Detroit Board of Education, *Proceedings of the Board of Education* (1900-1901).

39. *General Register University of Michigan* (1916).

40. Detroit Public Schools, *Education in Detroit* (1916).

41. National Education Association of the United States, Today's education (1923), Vol. 14. .... *M.S.T.A. Quarterly Review* (1920).

42. *Michigan education journal* (Volume 8, 1930).

43. *77th Annual Report of the Library Commissioners, Detroit Public Library* (1943-1944), 1945. .... *Michigan education journal* (Volume 8, 1930).

44. 1930 US Census.

45. Matihlde Weidemann, *Nature magazine* ("Letter to the Editor" v34 1941).

Source Citations

46. *77th Annual Report of the Library Commissioners, Detroit Public Library* (1943-1944).

47. Bob Strome, "Weidemann Family" (a five page type-written document). .... 1880 US Census. .... 1900 US Census. .... 1910 US Census. .... Michigan, Births and Christenings Index, 1867-1911 (ancestry.com).

48. *Detroit Free Press,* 6 August 1905.

49. Margery Haite's handwritten notes to Richard Swanson.

50. *Michigan Births, 1867-1902* (familysearch.org). .... 1880 US Census. .... Michigan, Births and Christenings Index, 1867-1911 (ancestry.com).

51. Bob Strome, "Weidemann Family" (a five page type-written document). .... 1900 US Census. .... 1880 US Census. .... 1910 US Census. .... 1930 US Census.

52. Letter of recommentation from Elysian Mfg. Co. in Mark Swanson Collection (1901).

53. City Directories for Detroit, Michigan (1905).

54. Bob Strome, "Weidemann Family" (a five page type-written document). .... Find-A-Grave (www.findagrave.com).

55. Bob Strome, "Weidemann Family" (a five page type-written document). .... Find-A-Grave (www.findagrave.com). .... Michigan Death Certificates, 1921-1952 (familysearch.org).

56. Find-A-Grave (www.findagrave.com).

57. New York State Census, 1865 (familysearch.org).

58. U.S., Indexed County Land Ownership Maps, 1860-1918 (ancestry.com).

59. Bob Strome, "Weidemann Family" (a five page type-written document). .... Michigan, Births and Christenings Index, 1867-1911 (ancestry.com). .... 1930 US Census.

60. *University of Michigan Student Directory* (1908).

61. Alma Swanson, *Personal letter to Emma Weidemann from Vassar in Mark Swanson collection* (July 3 1953).

62. *Detroit Free Press,* 10 Fe b 1936. .... Bob Strome, "Weidemann Family" (a five page type-written document).

63. *Michigan Births, 1867-1902* (familysearch.org). .... *World War I Draft Registration Cards, 1917-1918* (ancestry.com). .... 1910 US Census. .... 1900 US Census.

64. Michigan, Births and Christenings Index, 1867-1911 (ancestry.com).

65. Bob Strome, "Weidemann Family" (a five page type-written document). .... *Rootsweb Death Index, 1796-2010* (ancestry.com).

66. *World War I Draft Registration Cards, 1917-1918* (ancestry.com).

67. *The Evening Independent,* February 23, 1931.

68. *Detroit Free Press,* 10 Feb 1936. .... *Detroit Free Press,* 9 feb 1936.

Source Citations

69. *Detroit Free Press,* 9 Feb 1936.

70. *Detroit Free Press,* 10 Feb 1936.

71. 1940 US Census.

72. UK Census 1901.

73. Michigan Marriages, 1868-1925 (familysearch.org).

74. *Michigan, Marriages, 1868-1925* (familysearch.com).

75. 1900 US Census. .... Michigan, Death Certificates, 1921-1952 (familysearch.org).

76. Bob Strome, "Weidemann Family" (a five page type-written document). .... Michigan Marriages, 1868-1925 (familysearch.org). .... Michigan, Death Certificates, 1921-1952 (familysearch.org).

77. *Faucher Family Tree* (ancestry.com).

78. 1900 US Census. .... 1910 US Census.

79. *Faucher Family Tree* (ancestry.com). .... Social Security Death Index (ancestry.com). .... 1900 US Census. .... 1920 US Census. .... 1930 US Census.

80. Social Security Death Index (ancestry.com). .... *Rootsweb Death Index, 1796-2010* (ancestry.com).

81. Michigan Marriages, 1822-1995 (familysearch.org).

82. 1840 US Census.

83. Michigan, Death Records, 1897-1920 (ancestry.com).

84. Bob Strome, "Weidemann Family" (a five page type-written document). .... 1910 US Census. .... 1900 US Census. .... 1920 US Census. .... 1930 US Census. .... Michigan, Death Certificates, 1921-1952 (familysearch.org).

85. United States Social Security Death Index (familysearch.org).

86. United States Social Security Death Index (familysearch.org). .... Michigan Death Index, 1971-1996 (familysearch.com).

87. 1930 US Census. .... United States Social Security Death Index (familysearch.org). .... Michigan Death Index, 1971-1996 (familysearch.com).

88. *Pittsburgh Post-Gazette,* 29 Apr 1935.

89. Michigan, Marriage Records, 1867-1952 (ancestry.com).

90. 1930 US Census. .... Michigan, Marriage Records, 1867-1952 (ancestry.com).

91. California Death Records 1940-1997 (familysearch.org).

92. 8th grade certificate of completion for Oscar Weidemann.

93. U.S. Passport Applications, 1795-1925 (ancestry.com). .... *Detroit Free Press,* 20 Sep 1894.

94. Detroit City Directory 1891 (ancestry.com).

Source Citations

95. U.S. Passport Applications, 1795-1925 (ancestry.com).

96. Oscar Weidemann's expense notebook 1893-1894.

97. *Detroit Free Press,* 20 Sep 1894.

98. Hamburg Passenger Lists, 1850-1934 (ancestry.com). .... Margery Haite's handwritten notes to Richard Swanson.

99. Marriage certificate and record for Mary Monahan and Christian Weidemann (Erie County, NY, 1901). .... *Wm. P. Atkinson's Erie City Duplex 1901-1902* .

100. Wm. P. Atkinson's Erie City Duplex 1902-1903. .... *Wm. P. Atkinson's Erie City Duplex 1903-1904* . .... *Wm. P. Atkinson's Erie City Duplex 1904-1905* .

101. *The Detroit News* (9 Feb 1920), 9 Feb 1920.

102. *Detroit Free Press,* 10 Feb 1920.

103. *The Painter and Decorator* (Volume 36).

104. Death certificate, Wayne County, Michigan, Mary Weidemann; Detroit; 3378; 9 February 1920. .... Marriage certificate and record for Mary Monahan and Christian Weidemann (Erie County, NY, 1901).

105. Death certificate, Wayne County, Michigan, Mary Weidemann; Detroit; 3378; 9 February 1920.

106. New York, State Census, 1892 (familysearch.org), Albany, 07, 03.

107. Death certificate, Wayne County, Michigan.

108. Erie County Pennsylvania birth records. .... Bob Strome, "Weidemann Family" (a five page type-written document). .... 1910 US Census. .... Social Security Death Index (ancestry.com).

109. St. Andrews Catholic Church, Erie, Pennsylvania, baptism book.

110. Social Security Death Index (ancestry.com). .... *Web: Obituary Daily Times Index, 1995-2011* (ancestry.com).

111. Richard Swanson notes (written in margins of Wolff Family genealogy from Haite).

112. Margery Haite, "Wolff Family" (5 typewritten pages, circa 1978).

113. *Journal of proceedings of the Michigan Board of Education* (1928).

114. U.S. Public Records Index, Volume 2 (Ancestry.com).

115. *Vassar Pioneer Times,* Obituary Date: 2 Sep 2004.

116. Torbjörn Nikus, "Storkarhu Family" (2008, unpublish document).

117. Michigan Deaths, 1971-1996 (ancestry.com). .... Social Security Death Index (ancestry.com).

118. *Archives of Ophthalmology* (1988, http://archopht.ama-assn.org).

119. August Spångberg, *Stream of Time* (1966).

Source Citations

120. Germany, Select Births and Baptisms, 1558-1898 (ancestry.com).

121. Germany, Select Births and Baptisms, 1558-1898 (ancestry.com). .... Altenhagen Parish Records, 7/1835, p.301.

122. *Michigan City Dispatch,* 22 March 1906. .... Hamburg Passenger Lists, 1850-1934 (ancestry.com). .... Martin Sohn, email (2 Dec. 2010). .... Germany, Select Births and Baptisms, 1558-1898 (ancestry.com). .... Röckwitz Church Records, 1814.

123. Germany, Select Births and Baptisms, 1558-1898 (ancestry.com). .... Röckwitz Church Records, 1814.

124. Margery Haite's handwritten notes to Richard Swanson. .... Indiana Deaths, 1882-1920 (ancestry.com).

125. Jacob Piatt Dunn, *Indiana and Indianans* (1919).

126. Altenhagen Parish Records, 9/1829, p.814.

127. Martin Sohn, email (2 Dec. 2010).

128. Wayne County, Michigan Tract Books (familysearch.org).

129. 1860 US Census.

130. 1892 New Buffalo Master Directory (newbuffalogenes.com).

131. *Michigan City Dispatch,* 22 March 1906.

132. Margery Haite, "Wolff Family" (5 typewritten pages, circa 1978). .... 1900 US Census.

133. 1819 Mecklenburg-Schwerin Census (ancestry.com). .... *Michigan City News,* 23 Dec 1903. .... Kastorf (Stavenhagen) Chuch Records, 1811.

134. Kastorf (Stavenhagen) Chuch Records, 1811.

135. Margery Haite's handwritten notes to Richard Swanson. .... *Michigan Dispatch,* 17 Dec 1903. .... *Michigan City News,* 23 Dec 1903.

136. 1819 Mecklenburg-Schwerin Census (ancestry.com).

137. *Michigan Dispatch,* 17 Dec 1903.

138. *Michigan City News,* 23 Dec 1903.

139. 1880 US Census. .... Wayne County Michigan Death Records, 1897-1920.

140. Wayne County Michigan Death Records, 1897-1920. .... Cemetery Records Online (www.interment.net).

141. 1880 US Census. .... Wildberg Church Records, 1/1844, p.103.

142. Wildberg Church Records, 1/1844, p.103.

143. Michigan Marriages, 1851-1875 (ancestry.com). .... Margery Haite, "Wolff Family" (5 typewritten pages, circa 1978).

144. New York Passenger Lists, 1820-1957 (ancestry.com). .... Wildberg Church Records, 5/1846, p.111.

Source Citations

145. Wildberg Church Records, 5/1846, p.111.

146. *La Porte County News Dispatch* (1924). .... U.S. Naturalization Record Indexes, 1791-1992 (ancestry.com).

147. Greenwood Cemetery LaPorte (http://www.dunelady.com/laporte/cemeteries/greenwood). .... Find-A-Grave (www.findagrave.com).

148. Oklahoma, County Marriages, 1890-1995 (www.familysearch.com).

149. Michigan Marriage Records, 1822-1995 (familysearch.com). .... Wildberg Church Records, 46/1848, p.121.

150. Wildberg Church Records, 46/1848, p.121.

151. Michigan, Death Certificates, 1921-1952 (familysearch.org).

152. Michigan Marriage Records, 1822-1995 (familysearch.com).

153. Oklahoma Marriages, 1870-1930 (familysearch.com).

154. New York Passenger Lists, 1820-1957 (ancestry.com). .... Wildberg Church Records, 11/1852, p.135.

155. Wildberg Church Records, 11/1852, p.135.

156. 1870 US Census. .... New York Passenger Lists, 1820-1957 (ancestry.com). .... Wildberg Church Records, 12/1855, p.144.

157. Wildberg Church Records, 12/1855, p.144.

158. Montana Death Index, 1860-2007 (familysearch.org).

159. International Genealogical Index - North America (familysearch.org).

160. Montana, County Marriages, 1865-1950 (familysearch.org), daughter Maxine's marriage.

161. 1930 US Census. .... Montana, County Marriages, 1865-1950 (familysearch.org).

162. Michigan, Deaths and Burials Index, 1867-1995 (ancestry.com).

163. 1860 US Census. .... 1880 US Census. .... Cemetery Records Online (www.interment.net).

164. Cemetery Records Online (www.interment.net).

165. Find-A-Grave (www.findagrave.com). .... Michigan Death Certificates, 1921-1952 (familysearch.org).

166. Michigan, County Marriages, 1820-1940 (familysearch.org).

167. Cemetery Records Online (www.interment.net). .... Michigan Death Certificates, 1921-1952 (familysearch.org).

168. Michigan Births and Christenings, 1775-1995 (familysearch.org).

169. Michigan Death Certificates, 1921-1952 (familysearch.org).

170. 1880 US Census. .... 1870 US Census. .... Find-A-Grave (www.findagrave.com).

Source Citations

171. Texas, Death Certificates, 1903–1982 (ancestry.com). .... 1870 US Census.

172. Texas, Death Certificates, 1903–1982 (ancestry.com).

173. Missouri, County Marriage, Naturalization, and Court Records (familysearch.org).

174. 1910 US Census. .... Texas Deaths, 1890-1976 (familysearch.org).

175. Texas Deaths, 1890-1976 (familysearch.org).

176. 1870 US Census. .... Michigan Death Certificates, 1921-1952 (familysearch.org).

177. Michigan Marriages, 1868-1925 (familysearch.org). .... Michigan Death Certificates, 1921-1952 (familysearch.org).

178. Michigan, Death Records, 1867-1950 (ancestry.com). .... Michigan Death Certificates, 1921-1952 (familysearch.org).

179. Michigan, Births and Christenings Index, 1867-1911 (ancestry.com). .... Find-A-Grave (www.findagrave.com).

180. United States World War I Draft Registration Cards, 1917-1918 (familysearch.org).

181. 1880 US Census. .... Find-A-Grave (www.findagrave.com).

182. Find-A-Grave (www.findagrave.com). .... Michigan Marriages, 1822-1995 (familysearch.org).

183. Michigan, County Marriages, 1820-1940 (familysearch.org). .... United States World War I Draft Registration Cards, 1917-1918 (familysearch.org).

184. U.S. Naturalization Record Indexes, 1791-1992 (ancestry.com).

185. *La Porte County News Dispatch* (1924), 12 Jan 1924.

186. Illinois Marriages, 1851-1900 (ancestry.com).

187. Illinois Deaths and Stillbirths, 1916-1947 (familysearch.org).

188. Illinois Deaths and Stillbirths, 1916-1947 (familysearch.org). .... Indiana Marriages, 1811-2007 (familysearch.org).

189. Indiana, Death Index, 1882-1920.

190. Indiana Marriages, 1780-1992 (familysearch.org).

191. 1920 US Census. .... United States World War I Draft Registration Cards, 1917-1918 (familysearch.org).

192. 1920 US Census. .... 1900 US Census. .... United States Social Security Death Index (familysearch.org).

193. Ohio Births and Christenings (familysearch.org).

194. 1930 US Census. .... United States World War I Draft Registration Cards, 1917-1918 (familysearch.org). .... Ohio Births and Christenings (familysearch.org).

195. 1920 US Census. .... United States World War II Draft Registration Cards, 1942 (familysearch.org).

Source Citations

196. 1920 US Census. .... Find-A-Grave (www.findagrave.com). .... United States, GenealogyBank Obituaries, 1980-2014 (familysearch.org).

197. United States, GenealogyBank Obituaries, 1980-2014 (familysearch.org).

198. *Hartford Courant,* 15 August 1994.

199. Margery Haite, "Wolff Family" (5 typewritten pages, circa 1978). .... Michigan Marriages, 1868-1925 (familysearch.org).

200. Social Security Death Index (ancestry.com).

201. A. T. Andreas, *Historical Atlas of Dakota* (1884).

202. South Dakota, State Census, 1915 (ancestry.com).

203. Bureau of Land Management (BLM) (thelandpatents.com).

204. South Dakota State Census, 1905 (familysearch.org).

205. *The Daily Deadwood Pioneer-Times,* 7 September 1926.

206. 1900 US Census. .... California, Death Index, 1940-1997 (familysearch.org).

207. California, Death Index, 1940-1997 (familysearch.org). .... *Idaho State Journal from Pocatello, Idaho,* December 5, 1950.

208. *Idaho State Journal from Pocatello, Idaho,* December 5, 1950.

209. 1900 US Census. .... Michigan Death Records, 1897-1920 (seekingmichigan.com).

210. Ancestral File Number: 3DMZ-PMF (familysearch.org). .... Michigan Death Records, 1897-1920 (seekingmichigan.com).

211. 1910 US Census. .... South Dakota Births, 1856-1903 (ancestry.com).

212. U.S., Social Security Death Index, 1935-2014 (ancestry.com). .... State of Florida. Florida Death Index, 1877-1998 (ancestry.com).

213. *New York, Passenger Lists, 1820-1957* (ancestry.com).

214. *An illustrated history of the Yellowstone Valley* (Western Historical Publishing Co., 1907).

215. State of Montana Records (dnrc.mt.gov/divisions/water/water-rights/docs).

216. *The Billings Gazette from Billings, Montana,* 12 January 1928.

217. 1900 US Census. .... Spivak/Slaten Family Tree (ancestry.com).

218. Spivak/Slaten Family Tree (ancestry.com).

219. Montana, County Marriages, 1865-1950 (familysearch.org).

220. Minnesota Births and Christenings, 1840-1980 (familysearch.org).

221. 1930 US Census. .... Montana, County Marriages, 1865-1950 (familysearch.org). .... Find-A-Grave

Source Citations

(www.findagrave.com). .... Montana Death Index, 1860-2007 (familysearch.org). .... United States Social Security Death Index (familysearch.org).

222. Find-A-Grave (www.findagrave.com). .... United States Social Security Death Index (familysearch.org).

223. 1870 US Census. .... 1880 US Census.

224. Croom Parish records (registers.nli.ie).

225. Application Archive A0244(5)S(D8) (Weschester Historical Society).

226. New York, Census of Inmates in Almshouses and Poorhouses, 1830-1920 (Ancentry.com).

227. 1880 US Census. .... U.S. City Directories, 1821-1989 (ancestry.com).

228. *www.rootsireland.ie*. .... Croom Parish records (registers.nli.ie).

229. Albany Bureau of Vital Statistics. .... 1870 US Census.

230. Albany Bureau of Vital Statistics.

231. Troy Irish Genealogy Society Website (http://www.rootsweb.ancestry.com/).

232. 1870 US Census. .... Croom Parish Baptism Record (rootsireland.ie). .... Croom Parish records (registers.nli.ie).

233. *The Yonkers Statesman,* 4 October 1924.

234. Correspondence with Jim Logan, Superintendent, Sleepy Hollow Cemetery (2014).

235. Croom Parish Baptism Record (rootsireland.ie). .... 1870 US Census. .... Croom Parish records (registers.nli.ie).

236. New York, New York, Death Index, 1862-1948 (ancestry.com).

237. New York Passenger Lists, 1820-1957 (ancestry.com). .... 1830 US Census.

238. Croom Parish Baptism Record (rootsireland.ie). .... Croom Parish records (registers.nli.ie).

239. Croom Parish Baptism Record (rootsireland.ie). .... 1880 US Census. .... 1870 US Census. .... Croom Parish records (registers.nli.ie).

240. Massachusetts Deaths, 1841-1915 (familysearch.org).

241. Boston Passenger and Crew Lists, 1820-1943 (ancestry.com).

242. Baptism Record Church of Immaculate Conception Church, Westchester, New York (1868).

243. Ohio Deaths, 1908-1953 (familysearch.org).

244. 1880 US Census. .... Ohio Deaths, 1908-1953 (familysearch.org). .... *Stone Cutters' Journal*. .... City of Cleveland Register of Interments (www.rootsweb.ancestry.com).

245. City of Cleveland Register of Interments (www.rootsweb.ancestry.com). .... Ohio Deaths, 1908-1953 (familysearch.org).

Source Citations

246. Frederick Ludwig Hoffman, *Mortality from Respiratory Diseases in Dusty Trades (inorganic Dusts)* . .... Ohio Deaths, 1908-1953 (familysearch.org).

247. *Stone Cutters' Journal,* 1914-1915.

248. *Bloomington (Indiana) Weekly Courier,* May 11, 1915.

249. *Bloomington Evening World,* 8 September 1915.

250. *Stone Cutters' Journal,* 1922-1923.

251. 1830 US Census.

252. *Stone Cutters' Journal,* November 1938.

253. Indiana, Select Marriages, 1780-1992 (familysearch.org).

254. Kentucky, Marriage Records, 1852-1914 (ancestry.com).

255. Indiana, Select Marriages, 1780-1992 (familysearch.org). .... 1860 US Census. .... Keuruu, Rippikirja, 1712-1736 (sukuhistoria.fi). .... Kentucky Marriages, 1785-1979 (familysearch.org).

256. Ohio, County Marriages, 1789-1994 (familysearch.org). .... 1910 US Census.

257. Ohio, County Marriages, 1789-1994 (familysearch.org).

258. Find-A-Grave (www.findagrave.com). ....*Ohio, Deaths, 1908-1932, 1938-2007* (ancestry.com).

259. Connecticut Births and Christenings, 1649-1906 (familysearch.org).

260. New York, State Census, 1905 (familysearch.org).

261. New York, State Census, 1915 (ancestry.com).

262. *The Yonkers Statesman,* 4 Oct 1924.

263. New York, Find A Grave Index, 1664-2011 (ancestry.com).

264. New York, County Marriages, 1908-1935 (familysearch.org).

265. Ehles letter on Weidemann (24 April 1997 to Margery Haite). .... Wiebke Dannenberg, "The Weidemann Family from Stolpe, East-Holstein, Germany" (25 June 2005, unpublished document). .... Arbeitskreis (akvz.de).

266. Ehles letter on Weidemann (24 April 1997 to Margery Haite). .... Wiebke Dannenberg, "The Weidemann Family from Stolpe, East-Holstein, Germany" (25 June 2005, unpublished document).

267. Wiebke Dannenberg, "The Weidemann Family from Stolpe, East-Holstein, Germany" (25 June 2005, unpublished document). .... 1803 Klenau, Dorf parish census (http://www.danishfamilysearch.com/).

268. 1803 Klenau, Dorf parish census (http://www.danishfamilysearch.com/).

269. Altenhagen Parish Records, 7/1835, p.301.

270. Altenhagen Parish Records, Altenhagen, 7/1835, p.301.

271. Röckwitz Church Records, 1810.

Source Citations

272. Röckwitz Church Records, 1789.

273. Germany, Select Births and Baptisms, 1558-1898 (ancestry.com). .... Röckwitz Church Records, 1789.

274. Wolkow Church Records, 19/1861.

275. Kastorf (Stavenhagen) Chuch Records, 1782.

276. Kastorf (Stavenhagen) Chuch Records, 1757.

277. Röckwitz Church Records, 1821.

278. Borgfeld (Stavenhagen) Church Records, 15/1776.

279. Kastorf (Stavenhagen) Chuch Records, 1755.

280. Kastorf (Stavenhagen) Chuch Records, 4/1768.

281. Kastorf (Stavenhagen) Chuch Records, 1829.

282. Kastorf (Stavenhagen) Chuch Records, 1799.

283. Kastorf (Stavenhagen) Chuch Records, 1821.

284. Wolfgang Hohenfeld, GedBas: Die genealogische Datenbasis (http://www.gedbas.de). .... Wiebke Dannenberg, "The Weidemann Family from Stolpe, East-Holstein, Germany" (25 June 2005, unpublished document).

285. Wolfgang Hohenfeld, GedBas: Die genealogische Datenbasis (http://www.gedbas.de). .... Wiebke Dannenberg, "The Weidemann Family from Stolpe, East-Holstein, Germany" (25 June 2005, unpublished document). .... Website of Ilkka Westergren (myheritage.com).

286. Wolfgang Hohenfeld, GedBas: Die genealogische Datenbasis (http://www.gedbas.de).

287. Wolfgang Hohenfeld, GedBas: Die genealogische Datenbasis (http://www.gedbas.de). .... Website of Ilkka Westergren (myheritage.com).

288. Website of Ilkka Westergren (myheritage.com).

289. Arbeitskreis (akvz.de).

290. Wiebke Dannenberg, "The Weidemann Family from Stolpe, East-Holstein, Germany" (25 June 2005, unpublished document). .... Correspondence with Paul-Otto Irmert of Neustadt in Holstein, 11 February 2016. .... Arbeitskreis (akvz.de).

291. Wiebke Dannenberg, "The Weidemann Family from Stolpe, East-Holstein, Germany" (25 June 2005, unpublished document). .... Bob Strome, "Weidemann Family" (a five page type-written document).

292. Ostholstein, Germany, Lutheran Baptisms, Marriages, and Burials, 1597-1959 (in German) (ancestry.com).

293. Wiebke Dannenberg, "The Weidemann Family from Stolpe, East-Holstein, Germany" (25 June 2005, unpublished document). .... Hamburg, Germany, Deaths, 1874-1950 (ancestry.com).

294. Ehles letter on Weidemann (24 April 1997 to Margery Haite). .... Wiebke Dannenberg, "The Weidemann Family from Stolpe, East-Holstein, Germany" (25 June 2005, unpublished document). .... 1800 US Census.

Source Citations

295. William Stocking and Gordon K. Miller, *The City of Detroit, Michigan, 1701-1922* (Volume 5). .... Wiebke Dannenberg, "The Weidemann Family from Stolpe, East-Holstein, Germany" (25 June 2005, unpublished document).

296. William Stocking and Gordon K. Miller, *The City of Detroit, Michigan, 1701-1922* (Volume 5). .... Michigan, Death Records, 1897-1920 (ancestry.com).

297. Margery Haite, "Wolff Family" (5 typewritten pages, circa 1978). .... Kastorf (Stavenhagen) Chuch Records, 1832.

298. Kastorf (Stavenhagen) Chuch Records, 1832.

299. Kastorf (Stavenhagen) Chuch Records, 1833.

300. Indiana Deaths, 1882-1920 (ancestry.com).

301. Danish Family Search Website (danishfamilysearch.com).

302. Wiebke Dannenberg, "The Weidemann Family from Stolpe, East-Holstein, Germany" (25 June 2005, unpublished document). .... Ostholstein, Germany, Lutheran Baptisms, Marriages, and Burials, 1597-1959 (in German) (ancestry.com).

303. 1870 US Census. .... Wiebke Dannenberg, "The Weidemann Family from Stolpe, East-Holstein, Germany" (25 June 2005, unpublished document).

304. Röckwitz Church Records, 1812.

305. Altenhagen Parish Records, 13/1827. .... Germany, Select Births and Baptisms, 1558-1898 (ancestry.com). .... Röckwitz Church Records, 1812.

306. Altenhagen Parish Records, 17/1817, p.219.

307. Wolkow Church Records, 1/1844.

308. Altenhagen Parish Records, 13/1819, p.227.

309. Altenhagen Parish Records, 14/1827.

310. Altenhagen Parish Records, 1/1822, p.545.

311. Mecklenburg, Germany, Parish Register Transcripts, 1740-1918 (ancestry.com).

312. Altenhagen Parish Records.

313. Gültz Parish Records.

314. Röckwitz Church Records, 1/1861.

315. Correspondence with Janine Leifels (2014). .... Röckwitz Church Records, 1835.

316. Röckwitz Church Records, 1835.

317. Correspondence with Janine Leifels (2014).

318. Kastorf (Stavenhagen) Chuch Records, 1802.

Source Citations

319. Kastorf (Stavenhagen) Chuch Records, 1804.

320. 1819 Mecklenburg-Schwerin Census (ancestry.com). .... Kastorf (Stavenhagen) Chuch Records, 1804.

321. Kastorf (Stavenhagen) Chuch Records, 1806.

322. 1819 Mecklenburg-Schwerin Census (ancestry.com). .... Kastorf (Stavenhagen) Chuch Records, 1806.

323. Kastorf (Stavenhagen) Chuch Records, 1808. .... Find-A-Grave (www.findagrave.com).

324. 1819 Mecklenburg-Schwerin Census (ancestry.com). .... Kastorf (Stavenhagen) Chuch Records, 1808.

325. Kastorf (Stavenhagen) Chuch Records, 1808.

326. LDS Microfilm 69242, Kirchenbuch von Kastorf.

327. 1819 Mecklenburg-Schwerin Census (ancestry.com). .... Kastorf (Stavenhagen) Chuch Records, 1813.

328. Kastorf (Stavenhagen) Chuch Records, 1813.

329. 1819 Mecklenburg-Schwerin Census (ancestry.com). .... Kastorf (Stavenhagen) Chuch Records, 1816.

330. Kastorf (Stavenhagen) Chuch Records, 1816.

331. 1819 Mecklenburg-Schwerin Census (ancestry.com). .... Kastorf (Stavenhagen) Chuch Records, 1818.

332. Kastorf (Stavenhagen) Chuch Records, 1818.

333. Borgfeld Church Records, 15/1776.

334. Kastorf (Stavenhagen) Chuch Records, 1/1777.

335. Kastorf (Stavenhagen) Chuch Records, 1780.

336. Kastorf (Stavenhagen) Chuch Records, 6/1784.

337. Kastorf (Stavenhagen) Chuch Records, 1787.

338. Wolde Church Records, 1809.

339. Germany, Select Births and Baptisms, 1558-1898 (ancestry.com). .... Röckwitz Church Records, 1793.

340. Röckwitz Church Records, 1793.

341. Kastorf (Stavenhagen) Chuch Records, 19/1762.

342. Kastorf (Stavenhagen) Chuch Records, 11/1767.

343. Kastorf (Stavenhagen) Chuch Records, 4/1770.

344. Kastorf (Stavenhagen) Chuch Records, 18/1775.

345. Wiebke Dannenberg, "The Weidemann Family from Stolpe, East-Holstein, Germany" (25 June 2005, unpublished document). .... Danish Family Search Website (danishfamilysearch.com), 1803 Census.

346. Wolde Church Records, 1784.

Source Citations

347. Röckwitz Church Records, 1784.

348. Dethlefsen (StDethlefsen) Tree (ancestry.com).

Name Index

Name Index

Name Index

Name Index

Name Index

Name Index

Name Index

Name Index

Location Index

Location Index

Location Index

Location Index

Location Index

Location Index